THE
APPLE
COOKBOOK

OLWEN WOODIER

Garden Way Publishing
Pownal, Vermont 05261

Book design by Andrea Gray

Illustrations compiled or drawn by Andrea Gray and Leslie Fry

Printed in the United States by Alpine Press

Second Printing, July, 1985

Library of Congress Cataloging in Publication Data

Woodier, Olwen, 1942-
   The apple cookbook.

   Includes index.
   1. Cookery (Apples) I. Title.
TX813.A6W67   1984   641.6′411   83-48976
ISBN 0-88266-377-1
   0-88266-367-4 (pbk.)

CONTENTS

APPLE
FACTS

Man has been munching on apples for about 750,000 years, ever since the food gatherers of early Paleolithic times discovered sour, wild crab apples growing in the Caucasus Mountains in west Asia. Later, apples were first cultivated by Neolithic farmers; and the carbonized remains unearthed in Asia Minor indicate this to be around 8,000 years ago.

There is recorded evidence from 1300 B.C. of apple orchards being planted along the Nile Delta. From there it was just a short hop on the trade routes to Greece and Italy where cultivated apple varieties were in great demand.

Colonists arriving in America found only four varieties of wild crab apples. However, the French, Dutch, German, and English had all brought seeds from their homelands, and it wasn't long before apple trees were growing outside their rustic dwellings.

The first orchard was planted in Boston in 1625 by William Blaxton, an English preacher. A few years later, orchards were established in the same area by John Winthrop and John Endecott, governors of the Bay Colony settlement.

In 1647, Peter Stuyvesant, governor of New Amsterdam (now New York), planted the first Dutch apple trees on his farm, The Bouwerie. The first commercial orchard was planted in Flushing, Long Island, in 1730.

As the colonists moved from the Atlantic coast westward, they planted apple seeds along the way. The most famous apple seed sower was John Chapman, or Johnny Appleseed as everyone came to know him. Born in 1774, in Massachusetts, he left home at an early age to follow the pioneers to the new frontiers with the intention of teaching the Bible and planting apple nurseries from seeds. This mission he accomplished, and when he died in Indiana, in 1854, he was doing his customary rounds of his many apple trees.

Favorably influenced by the moderately cool winters, the colonists' apple crops flourished in the northern regions. Apples, just like autumn leaves, need the perfect marriage of temperatures—warm, sunny days and cool nights that occur in October—to show off their best qualities. It is during this time that the apple greens change into dazzling reds, yellows, and golds. Even the greenish-yellows, purple-reds, browns, and mottles blend into those rich hues that seem to embody the spirit of autumn.

October positively sings of apples and autumn. No wonder that the apple connoisseurs have turned it into National Apple Month. A visit to the orchards at this time of year is a wonderful assault on the senses. The soft autumn days are redolent with the winey fragrance of ripe fruit and the woody smell of smoke that lingers in the damp air.

AMERICA'S NUMBER ONE FRUIT

The states that have emerged as the main apple-growing regions include Washington, New York, Michigan, Pennsylvania, California, Virginia, and North Carolina, in that order. Out of the forty apple-growing states, these seven areas are responsible for producing 60 percent of the country's annual apple crop, which totaled 193 million bushels in 1982. One-third of that crop is grown to be processed into canned, frozen, and dehydrated products.

It's not only their year-round availability that makes apples so desirable in the United States; there are a host of other reasons why they're America's number one fruit. For those who are weight conscious, apples make a great snack by providing satisfying bulk and few calories—a medium-size 2¾-inch apple contains only eighty or so calories.

Another good thing about apples is that they're 85–95 percent water, so if you put one in your pocket or lunch box, you can quench your thirst whenever the need arises. Their acid content acts as a natural mouth freshener, which makes eating apples a perfect ending to a meal. In fact, if you want to keep your children's teeth really healthy, slip an apple into every lunch box you pack. Studies have shown that children who snack on apples have fewer cavities than those who snack on candy, sticky dried fruits, and soft drinks.

Apples contain traces of vitamins A and B, and moderate amounts of calcium, iron, and phosphorus. The high pectin and malic acid present in a raw apple help promote good digestion and elimination. Don't remove the skin though; it helps furnish essential dietary fiber.

When you eat a recently picked, sun-kissed apple with the skin intact, you also consume 22 milligrams of vitamin C. If you peel that apple, you lose about 8 milligrams of vitamin C. Later on, when apples come out of storage, the vitamin C will be less than 14 milligrams, even with the skin left on. If you peel such an apple, you'll reduce the vitamin C by about half.

During the 1970s, researchers at Michigan State University carried out a study on their students. Those eating two apples a day suffered fewer headaches and respiratory illnesses, and had better health in general, than the students who ate none.

Nutritive Value of a 2¾-Inch, 150-Gram Raw Apple With Skin*

Water	84.4	percent
Calories	80	
Protein	.3	grams
Fat	.8	grams
Carbohydrates	20	grams
Calcium	10	milligrams
Phosphorus	14	milligrams
Iron	.4	milligrams
Sodium	1	milligram
Potassium	152	milligrams
Vitamin A	120	International Units
Vitamin B		
Thiamin	.04	milligrams
Riboflavin	.03	milligrams
Niacin	.1	milligrams
Vitamin C (ascorbic acid)	6	milligrams

*SOURCE: *USDA Handbook 456, Nutritive Value of American Foods*

If that's not good enough reason to eat an apple a day, perhaps the Rutgers 1975 report will convince skeptics. It showed that fruit pectins trap and prevent cholesterol from building up in the linings of blood vessel walls. This results in lowered blood pressure and reduced atherosclerosis symptoms.

When Eve was tempted by the serpent in the Garden of Eden to eat " . . . of the tree which is forbidden . . . " (forbidden because " . . . your eyes shall be opened and ye shall be as gods, knowing good and evil . . . "), she " . . . saw that the tree was good for food, and that it was pleasant to the eyes, and a tree to be desired to make one wise . . . " No doubt, she was also quite taken by the shape, color, and smell of this "fruit of the gods."

Imagine yourself picking up an apple for the very first time. Turn it around in your hand. If it's one of the russet apples, it will feel rough and dry, not at all like a red-on-yellow Empire with its satiny smooth and tender skin. Hold it to your nose and breathe deeply. The smooth-skinned Empire will have a delicate smell that is well contained by its smooth and slightly oily skin. The rough skin of a ripe russet, on the other hand, will exude a tantalizing fragrance.

Most of the perfume cells are concentrated in the skin of an apple. As the apple ripens, the cells give off a stronger aroma. This is why apple sauce is most flavorful when made from apples with the skin left on. For the same reason, the best cider is made from the aromatic, tough-skinned russets.

Rosy pink apple sauce gets its color from the flesh, not from the skin—unless the skin has been pureed with the flesh to become an integral part of the sauce. The pigments trapped in the skin cells are not released during cooking, crushing, or pressing because those color cells are impossible to break.

Apple trees have not only taken the fancy of gods and mortals, they attract over thirty species of birds and a variety of four-legged animals. There are birds who love to nest in the spreading branches. Many birds and beasts feast on the buds, bark, and leaves. The ripe, fallen apples are favored by porcupines, skunks, fox, and deer. Possums, raccoons, bears, and children all climb the limbs to get at apple-laden branches.

POPULAR ORCHARD VARIETIES

Although at least 300 varieties of apple are grown in America, only 20 or so are cultivated in the major commercial orchards. Commercial apples are not chosen for their wonderful taste, but for their bountiful harvest; their suitability to mass planting, shipping, and long storage; and their resistance to diseases.

The orchards are invaded by armies of apple pickers as early as July, but it is not until the cooler temperatures of September have touched this "fruit of immortality," as it was once called, that an apple takes on those crisp and crunchy qualities deemed so important to orchardists and apple lovers. It is in autumn that a bite into a fresh-picked apple becomes a memorable experience when it spurts juice that is honey sweet and yet also spicily tart, and the flesh is so fragrantly mellow.

After December, these fall beauties come to us from controlled storage—somewhere between thirty-two and thirty-six degrees Fahrenheit. As the year wears on, the delicious fresh qualities of the apples deteriorate. From January through June, most shoppers find they are limited to five stalwart keepers —Red Delicious, Golden Delicious, McIntosh, Rome Beauty, and Granny Smith. (Although Granny Smith apples are grown in the United States, most of those we eat come from Australia.)

Storage apples generally have been rinsed in a mild detergent and are often treated with chemicals to prevent dark spots from developing. The Red and Golden Delicious apples that are shipped from Washington state are usually coated with a vegetable wax to replace the natural wax removed during the washing process.

The following descriptions cover those apple varieties that are the most popular with the orchardists, are good keepers, and are available for several months in a number of states.

The descriptions of the general characteristics should be taken as just that, general. Like wines, the quality of apples depends on many factors—latitude, terrain, weather, and the care with which they were grown, among others.

Apples of the same variety vary not only from year to year, but from day to day, as they mature. I've had apples from the same bag, in fact, that varied widely in appearance and taste. Maybe they were the same shape, but the colors were remarkably different, depending on the degree of ripeness.

The background, or undercast, color of an apple changes from dark green to light green to yellow as it ripens, and the surface turns a bright red or a deeper yellow. In some apples, the surface color completely obscures the background color. Take, for example, my favorite apple, the Empire. Sometimes these are all bright red, sometimes bright red on a yellow background. A knock-out of juicy spiciness when fully mature, the Empire is flat and uninteresting when eaten before its prime.

Some apples at first look are only a solid green, yellow, or red; but on closer inspection, it can often be seen that they are faintly streaked, marbled, or dotted with a yellow or pink blush. So, as I have said, descriptions of apples can be at best just general.

Cortland. This apple, a cross between a Ben Davis and a McIntosh, was developed by the New York Agricultural Experiment Station in Geneva, New York. It entered the commercial market in 1915. Cortlands are grown mainly in the Northeast, the northern Great Lakes states, Ontario, and eastern Canada. A medium-to-large red-and-green-striped apple, it is crisp, juicy, and sweetly tart. Because its white flesh resists browning, Cortlands are favored for salads and fruit cups. It is also a good all-purpose apple.

Golden Delicious. Grown in most regions across the country, Golden Delicious is rated the second best seller after Red Delicious, to which it is not related at all. The Golden Delicious (or Yellow Delicious as it is sometimes called) was discovered in West Virginia in 1914, when it was called Mullin's Yellow Seedling. It was later purchased by the Stark Brothers. This is a medium-to-large pale yellow or yellow green apple that is mild and sweet. Although it is crisp when harvested in September and October, its pale flesh often becomes dry and soft. Its skin shrivels when not kept under refrigeration. Particularly desirable for snacks, fresh desserts, and salads, the Golden Delicious is a good all-purpose apple.

Red Delicious. Grown throughout the United States, the Red Delicious is America's most popular apple. First called Hawkeye when it was discovered in 1872 in Peru, Iowa, its name was changed to Red Delicious in 1895 by the Stark Brothers. This bright red apple is crisp and juicy when harvested in September and October. Although Red Delicious is considered a good keeper by the industry, its sweet and mild-tasting flesh is all too often a mealy, mushy disappointment. It is best used for snacks, salads, and fruit cups.

Empire. A cross between Red Delicious and McIntosh, the Empire was introduced into commercial production by the New York Agricultural Experiment Station in Geneva, New York, in 1966. Grown mostly in the Northeast and upper midwestern states, this medium-size, red-on-yellow (sometimes all red) apple is crisp and juicy. With its sweet and spicy flesh, it is one of the very best for eating out of hand, in salads, and in fruit cups.

Idared. This apple was scientifically developed in 1942 at the University of Idaho Agricultural Experiment Station. It is a cross between a Jonathan and a Wagener. Although grown in greatest volume in the northeastern and upper midwestern states, its production is increasing by popular demand throughout the country. It is medium-to-large, bright red, and has creamy-white flesh that is very firm, crisp, and juicy. All-purpose apples, the sweetly tart, deliciously spicy Idareds are especially good for snacks and desserts, and their firm quality makes them particularly

desirable for baking. The flavor improves after several months in controlled atmosphere storage.

Jerseymac. A medium-to-large, red apple with a green undercast. Its tough skin encases flesh that is tangy, crunchy, and juicy. Although it makes a good all-purpose apple, it does not keep well.

Jonamac. A small-to-medium, red-on-green apple that is firm, mildly tart, and juicy. This can be considered an all-purpose apple; however, it is not a good keeper.

Jonathan. This was called Rick Apple when it was first discovered in 1820 at Woodstock, New York. Although it is the fifth-largest apple crop in the United States, its production in the North is now limited. It is a medium-size red apple with an attractive yellow blush. The flesh is firm, crisp, juicy, and sweetly tart, with a spicy aftertaste. Jonathan is a great all-purpose apple and, because it holds its shape so well, is in demand for baking whole and in pies.

Lodi. A small-to-medium light green apple. Its firm flesh is mildly tart but rather flavorless. It is fine for cooking purposes, but it is not a good keeper.

McIntosh. John McIntosh discovered this apple in Ontario, Canada, in 1830. Ranking third in volume in the United States, it is grown throughout the northeastern and upper Great Lakes states, eastern Canada, and British Columbia. It is a medium-size red-on-green apple, with sweet flesh that is crisp, juicy, and slightly perfumed. Excellent to eat fresh in autumn; later, Macs are best used for sauce. McIntosh apples collapse when baked whole or in pies.

Macoun. A cross between a McIntosh and a Jersey Black, this is a medium-size red apple that sometimes has an unattractive grey bloom. However, its snow-white flesh is super crisp and juicy, and its honey sweetness makes up for its mild flavor. This is most desirable for eating fresh, for snacks, salads, and fruit cups. It also makes good apple sauce. A poor keeper—it gets soft and loses flavor in storage—it is rarely available after November. Macoun is grown mostly in the Northeast, with limited production in the northern Midwest.

Melrose. In 1970, the Ohio State Horticultural Society named Melrose the official state apple. It has a somewhat flat shape, and the skin is a dull red-on-yellow. However, it makes up for its drab appearance with firm, crisp flesh that is sweet, juicy, and flavorful. Melrose is an excellent all-purpose apple.

Mutsu. In 1948, the Japanese introduced this descendant of Golden Delicious into the United States. Although grown mostly in the Northeast, Mutsus are gaining in wider popularity. The very large yellow-green fruits are not unlike the Golden Delicious; however, the flesh is much juicier and coarser, and its skin suffers less from storage. It is an excellent all-purpose apple.

Newtown Pippin. Supposedly discovered in Newtown, Long Island, in the early 1700s, this is one of the oldest varieties to be found in commercial production. Grown mostly in California and Oregon, it is a great favorite with the processing industry—its firm, crisp, juicy, and sweetly tart flesh makes it ideal for pie fillings and sauce.

Northern Spy. This apple originated at East Bloomfield, New York, around 1800. Today, it is grown mostly throughout the Northeast, the northern Midwest, and eastern Canada. This is a medium-to-large apple with a pale green-to-yellow undercast, heavily striped with red. Its mellow, creamy flesh is crisp, juicy, and richly aromatic—qualities that are prized by the commercial processing industry. It is an excellent all-purpose apple and freezes well. Because it is a biennial bearer, Northern Spy is declining in popularity with commercial orchardists.

Patricia. A star. This is so limited in production that it sells out very quickly during the second week of September. One of the very best eaters, but not a good keeper, it is a small, light green and yellow apple splashed with pink. It is crisp, crunchy, juicy, sweet, and tastes of "apple."

Paulared. This variety was discovered in 1960, in Sparta, Michigan, and introduced commercially in 1967. It is grown mostly in the Northeast and northern Midwest states. A medium-size, early September apple, it is usually red, though sometimes shaded with yellow-green. The flesh is crisp, juicy, and sweetly tart. Although Paulareds are fair all-purpose apples, they are not good keepers and should be used within six weeks or so of harvest.

Puritan. A lemony yellow and pinkish apple that has firm, juicy, and puckery-tart flesh. Puritans are considered fair for all culinary uses, except for baking whole.

Raritan. This red-on-green apple has a great "apple" flavor and is one of my all-time favorites. It has wondrously crunchy, juice-spurting flesh that is mildly tart-sweet. It is a great thirst quencher.

Rome Beauty. This large deep red apple was found growing in Rome, Ohio, in 1816. The flesh is sweet, mildly tart, dry, and firm. Although mediocre for eating fresh, Rome Beauties are very good for baking because they retain their shape and flavor. For this

Apple Varieties and Their Best Uses

This table includes several antique apple varieties.
For more information on antique apples, see pages 149–152.

VARIETY	HARVEST AND AVAILABILITY	EATING	SALAD	SAUCE	BAKING WHOLE	PIE	FROZEN
Baldwin	Nov./April	Good	Good	Good	Good	Good	Fair
Cortland	Sept./June	Good	Excellent	Good	Good	Good	Fair
Golden Delicious	Sept./June	Good	Excellent	Excellent	Good	Good	Good
Red Delicious	Sept./June	Good	Good	Poor	Poor	Poor	Poor
Empire	Oct./June	Excellent	Good	Good	Fair	Fair	Fair
Idared	Oct./March	Good	Good	Good	Excellent	Excellent	Good
Jerseymac	Aug./Sept.	Good	Good	Good	Fair	Fair	Poor
Jonagold	Oct./April	Excellent	Excellent	Good	Good	Good	Good
Jonamac	Sept./Oct.	Good	Good	Good	Poor	Fair	Poor
Jonathan	Sept./April	Excellent	Good	Good	Excellent	Excellent	Good
Lodi	July/Aug.	Fair	Fair	Fair	Fair	Fair	Poor
McIntosh	Sept./June	Good	Fair	Good	Poor	Fair	Poor
Macoun	Sept./Nov.	Excellent	Good	Good	Poor	Fair	Poor
Melrose	Oct./April	Good	Good	Excellent	Excellent	Excellent	Excellent
Mutsu	Oct./May	Excellent	Good	Excellent	Good	Excellent	Good
Newton Pippin	Oct./May	Good	Good	Excellent	Good	Excellent	Good
Northern Spy	Oct./May	Good	Good	Good	Excellent	Excellent	Good
Patricia	Sept.	Excellent	Good	Good	Poor	Fair	Poor
Paulared	Sept./Oct.	Good	Good	Good	Fair	Fair	Poor
Puritan	Aug./Sept.	Poor	Fair	Fair	Poor	Fair	Poor
Raritan	August	Excellent	Good	Good	Poor	Fair	Poor
Rhode Island Greening	Oct./April	Poor	Fair	Good	Good	Good	Good
Rome Beauty	Oct./June	Poor	Fair	Good	Good	Good	Good
Granny Smith	Oct./June	Good	Good	Fair	Good	Good	Good
Stayman	Oct./May	Good	Good	Good	Good	Good	Good
Twenty Ounce	Aug./Dec.	Poor	Fair	Good	Good	Good	Good
Tydeman Red	Aug./Sept.	Fair	Fair	Fair	Poor	Fair	Poor
Wellington	Aug./Sept.	Good	Good	Good	Poor	Fair	Fair
Winesap	Nov./July	Excellent	Excellent	Excellent	Good	Good	Good
York Imperial	Oct./June	Excellent	Good	Good	Excellent	Excellent	Good

reason it has become the fourth most popular variety grown throughout the United States.

Granny Smith. Although one of the most popular varieties sold in the United States, it is imported here year-round from the Southern Hemisphere. Granny Smith originated in Sydney, Australia, about 100 years ago, and is now grown in California and Washington. It is a medium-size pale green apple that, depending on maturity, is mildly to very tart. It is crisp and firm, and even though it doesn't have great flavor, its rather hard flesh makes it a good all-purpose apple. The United States' crop is available October through June.

Stayman. Discovered by Dr. Stayman in Leavenworth, Kansas, in 1866, Stayman apples originated from Winesap seed; for that reason they are sometimes incorrectly called Stayman Winesap. Grown in the Northeast, eastern Midwest, and South Atlantic states, Stayman is a medium-large deep red apple, often shaded with green (it sometimes fails to ripen in the Northeast). Its sweetly tart flesh is crisp and juicy and is delicious for eating fresh. It is also a good all-purpose apple.

Tydeman Red. The skin of this red-on-green apple is tough and firm; the rather chewy flesh is on the tart side. A good cooking apple.

Wellington. A medium-size red-and-green apple with firm, somewhat juicy flesh. It is nothing spectacular, but a good all-purpose apple.

Winesap. Thought to have originated in New Jersey in the late 1700s, it is one of our oldest apples still in commercial production (Newtown Pippin is the other). Grown in most apple-producing regions, its heaviest volume comes from the Northwest and the Mid-Atlantic states. Of medium size, Winesap has thick red skin and crisp, crunchy, and juicy flesh. The flavor is sweetly tart with a winey aftertaste. Winesap is an excellent all-purpose apple.

York Imperial. When this apple was first discovered at York, Pennsylvania, around 1830, it was called Johnson's Fine Winter Apple. Grown in the Appalachian states of Pennsylvania, West Virginia, Virginia, Maryland, and Delaware, its production volume is high enough to rank it sixth in the United States. An apple of medium size with a lopsided shape, its skin is deep red with greenish yellow streaking. A crispy, firm apple that is both sweet and tart with a somewhat mild flavor, it is in great demand for commercial processing into pie filling and sauce. It is a good all-purpose apple which mellows in cold storage.

BUYING APPLES

Apples are available all year-round in North America. Obviously, weather and latitude play a big role in the distribution of apple orchards across the United States. Varieties that ripen in September in the southern states, ripen around November in the North. Because of differences in the climates, an apple variety that tastes sweet and perfumed in Vermont may be flat and mealy in Virginia. In fact, in the North, some apples must be picked before they are mature in order to beat the first frost. However, whatever the region, apples that are considered "best keepers" are left to ripen—often they become sweeter and more flavorful with age—in controlled-atmosphere storage at the larger commercial orchards.

Unfortunately, after December, the apples that reach the consumers are often transported long distances, left sitting around, and are not kept under refrigeration in the grocery stores or supermarkets. Some stores polish their apples to make them look even more appealing, and this removes the natural bloom. Once this bloom is removed, apples start to break down.

At the orchards, the loads of just-picked apples are so fresh and in such peak condition they haven't had *time* to bruise. It is for this reason that apple devotees go a little crazy every autumn. Starting as early as August sometimes and continuing through November, they make weekend pilgrimages to their local orchards and farm stands, looking for varieties that never reach the village markets or for those orchard jewels of limited production—such as Patricia and Raritan.

If you are interested in getting the freshest apples you can buy, then picking your own is the way to go. Not only are the apples less expensive, but you may end up with the sweetest, crunchiest, and juiciest apples you've ever had the pleasure of eating. Apple picking makes a great family outing, especially if you take a picnic along. To find out where you can pick your own apples, contact your local orchardists (they advertise in the Yellow Pages and the local newspapers) or call your county extension agent of the Department of Agriculture.

RATING APPLES

There's nothing mystical about choosing apples. As a rule, what you see is what you get. Not that you have to analyze each apple, but if you bear the following points in mind, you'll end up with some pretty good specimens in your bag.

Look for those that are bruise-free and firm to the touch. A bruise or blemish on the skin means a decay spot in the flesh.

Overripe apples will feel soft and the texture will be mealy or mushy. The background, or undercast, color will be a dull yellow or a dull green, instead of a soft light green or yellow.

When the green of an apple is very dark, it is an indication that the apple is not fully mature. Such apples will be hard, sour, and have poor flavor. Underripe apples are fine for cooking. If you want them for eating out of hand, refrigerate them and allow them to ripen slowly for a week or two.

It's not always easy to choose the perfect apple. Apples differ in color depending on the variety as well as their point of maturity. They may be bright green and red, solid vibrant red, golden-yellow, lemon-yellow, and even greenish-yellow. You may choose those that are striped red and green, or prefer a plain vivid green. And, whatever you do, don't pass by the russet apples with their mottled and rough skins. They may not win any beauty prizes, but their flavor can be divine.

11

Your decision to choose a particular variety should be influenced by what you plan to do with the apples. If they are for the lunch box, then you'll want crisp, crunchy, juicy apples. Summer apples that have these qualities include Raritan, Jonamac, Early Blaze, Patricia, and Paulared. Later, I would choose Empire, Jonagold, Mutsu, Macoun, and McIntosh, among others. If you want to bake apples whole, or make pies, then choose those that hold their shape and retain their flavor, such as Northern Spy, Stayman, and Jonathan. (For a complete breakdown of best uses for apples, refer to the table on page 9.)

Although most apples are sold loose by the pound, quart, peck, or bushel, some retail stores sell them packaged in perforated, plastic bags. The bags are stamped with the weight, variety, and the U.S. grade—U.S. Extra Fancy, U.S. Fancy, with U.S. No. 1 meeting the minimum standards of quality.

Apples are graded mostly according to color and size. A very large, deep red Red Delicious will be Extra Fancy, while a small, somewhat greenish Red Delicious will be U.S. No. 1. I am frequently disappointed by large, perfect-looking apples. All too often they turn out to be tasteless and mealy.

The orchardists who sell locally grade their apples somewhat differently. Extra Fancy becomes Grade A, and Fancy is called Grade B, seconds, or "utility." Grade B apples are those that grow on the inside of the tree and are not as colorful, as large, and sometimes not as sweet. Windfalls or bruised apples are also called "utility" or Grade 3.

When buying just enough apples for a pie, 2½ pounds will do it—that's about five large, seven to eight medium-size, or nine to ten small apples. A medium-size apple is approximately three inches in diameter.

A peck of apples weighs 10½ pounds, and there are 42 pounds in a bushel. It's cheaper to buy a bushel, but if you don't plan to go on an immediate cooking spree (this quantity would make about sixteen pies or twenty quarts of apple sauce), make sure you can store them until you're ready to use them, or that you have plenty of apple-loving friends.

STORING APPLES

Apples ripen ten times faster in a dry, warm atmosphere, than when they are in cold storage. For this reason, commercial orchardists store their apples in controlled-atmosphere (CA) sealed chambers. CA storage reduces (without arresting) an apple's intake of oxygen, which slows down its maturation process. This method prolongs the storage life of an apple by several months, and enables the orchardists to pick apples that are not meant for immediate consumption, before they are fully ripe. As they mature, ever so slowly, in CA storage, the good keepers retain their juicy, crisp texture while becoming more flavorful and sweeter.

The International Apple Institute advises consumers to keep their apples under refrigeration in the hydrator drawer, at temperatures anywhere from 32°F. to 40°F. Some apples, such as Mutsu and Northern

Spy, keep better at 38°F., while others, like Jonathan and Roxbury Russet, keep better at near freezing. Such cold storage helps to preserve the pectin, which gives the apple its firm flesh, and the vitamin C content.

The best apples for keeping include Cortland, Delicious, Empire, Idared, McIntosh, Macoun, Mutsu, Northern Spy, Rhode Island Greening, Rome Beauty, Granny Smith, Stayman, and Winesap. Summer apples harvested in July, August, and early September are not good keepers. These must be refrigerated immediately and used within four to six weeks. These include the following varieties: Lodi, Jerseymac, Jonamac, Paulared, Patricia, Puritan, Raritan, Tydeman Red, and Wellington. For descriptions of all these apples, refer to the section on Popular Apple Varieties, pages 5–10.

When keeping your apples under refrigeration, be sure to store them in perforated plastic bags or containers to prevent them from drying out. If you have a root cellar, crawl space, or garage that doesn't freeze, stack the apples in polyethylene-lined crates, or load them in plastic-lined baskets and then cover with polyethylene. The plastic not only prevents moisture loss, it slows down the apples' breathing process and protects them from absorbing such flavors as onions and garlic, which might also be stored in the vicinity. To provide insulation from frost, set the apple crates on several layers of newspapers and cover with blankets, burlap, or more newspapers during the colder months.

Apples stored in plastic bags or containers without holes must be opened once a week or so to release some of the accumulated gases and carbon dioxide. As the enclosed fruit absorbs oxygen, it exhales carbon dioxide, water vapor, and ethylene and other gases. Too much carbon dioxide causes the flesh to turn brown and mushy, and too much ethylene gas softens the skin. Ethylene also causes potatoes to sprout, so don't store apples near them.

With some varieties, even short exposure to warm temperatures causes overripening, a mealy texture, and loss of flavor. So, whether you pick your own apples or buy them in a store, put them in a cool place without delay. However, check first for damaged or bruised apples and set those aside for immediate use. As we all know, a rotten apple in the barrel surely does spoil the whole crop.

Besides refrigeration, other methods of preserving a bounteous harvest include freezing and canning slices and sauce, and putting up preserves, such as jams, jellies, butters, and chutney. For more information on these techniques, refer to Preserving the Apple Harvest, pages 131–146.

COOKING
WITH APPLES

As famous as apples are for pie, cooking with apples does not stop there. With even just a little imagination you can use this versatile fruit in almost as many savory recipes as there are dessert dishes.

Sliced into rings, apples can be sautéed along with pork chops and cider. Chopped and sautéed with onions, they elevate such pedestrian fare as braised cabbage and Polish sausage from Sunday's supper to a guest dish. When diced large, they make a delicious addition to any braised chicken recipe or pork and lamb stews. At sometime or another, we've all had one of the many variations of apple stuffing with turkey and duck. Apple chutneys, relishes, and sauces may also take their place next to pork, poultry, goose, game, and curries.

For dessert, apples can be stuffed and baked, crisply frittered, folded into crêpes, mixed into cakes and breads, baked in tarts and pies, and hidden in cobblers, crisps, crunches, and brown Betties.

APPLE TIPS

When cooking with apples, it's handy to know that:
- 1 pound of apples yields 4 cups when chopped or sliced and 1½ cups of apple sauce.
- 1 pound of apples may contain 4 small, 3 medium-size, or 2 large apples.
- Apple juice and apple cider can be used interchangeably in recipes.

Apple Equivalents

SIZE	DIAMETER IN INCHES	SLICED OR CHOPPED	GRATED	FINELY CHOPPED	SAUCE
Large	3¾	2 cups	1¼ cups	1½ cups	¾ cup
Medium	2¾	1⅓ cups	¾ cup	1 cup	½ cup
Small	2¼	¾ cup	½ cup	¾ cup	⅓ cup

- 2–2½ pounds of apples will suffice for a 9-inch or 10-inch pie. That means 8–9 small apples, 6–7 medium-size apples, or 4–5 large ones.
- Overripe apples, once the bruises have been removed, make good apple sauce or cider.
- When a recipe calls for tart apples, good choices are Granny Smith, Puritan, Twenty Ounce, Rhode Island Greening, Tydeman Red, Lodi, Jonamac, and Jerseymac. Underripe apples also may be used.
- Underripe apples can be chopped, diced, sliced, and grated for sautéing with vegetables or for putting in cakes, muffins, pies, and other cooked dishes.
- Sliced or cut apples will stay whiter longer if dropped in a bowl of water containing 2 tablespoons of lemon juice. (Cortland and Golden Delicious do not discolor as quickly as other varieties.)
- When recipes call for unpeeled apples, the apples always should be washed first. This not only ensures the removal of dirt accumulated during handling and transportation, but eliminates the possibility of pesticide consumption.

17

If you're peeling, coring, and slicing apples in quantity, you might find it useful to acquire an apple peeler that also cores. I use a colonial-type (old-fashioned) corer and a small paring knife to peel my apples, so I can't give a recommendation on any of the hand-cranked peelers that affix to the counter. However, in *The Busy Person's Guide to Preserving Food* (available from Garden Way Publishing), Janet Chadwick recommends the Nor-Pro which, she says, " . . . peeled, sliced, and cored; and although the blade requires a little guidance, I found that it did a good job . . . " She also mentions the Johnny Apple Peeler and the White Mountain Apple Peeler, both of which slice and core. All sell for about $20.

To Peel or Not to Peel

There's a lot of goodness in the peel of an apple. It contains vitamin C, fiber, and much of the apple's flavor. So why not leave the skin on for all the recipes? Because some apples have tough skins; and even if the skin is not tough when the apple is eaten raw, it does not break down in the cooking process. Nothing, in my opinion, spoils a fine cake, pudding, or apple sauce more than finding some cooked apple skin. By all means, you may leave the apple skins on in any of the recipes that call for peeling. Then see how you feel about "to peel or not to peel."

Planning to make gallons of apple sauce? Then you may want to invest in a special strainer. Heavy-duty strainers include the Victorio and the Garden Way Squeezo® Strainer. For small batches of sauce, a simple Foley food mill does a fine job.

If a recipe calls for a lot of chopped or grated vegetables and apples, I use a food processor. When a recipe calls for cubed apples though, I always prepare by hand to make sure I get uniform pieces. However, a food processor will make very thin and very uniform apple *slices* in no time at all.

I have given apple variety recommendations in most of the recipes in this cookbook because some recipes work better with sweet apples, some with tart apples, some with those apples that have a hard texture and don't fall apart. For example, in the Apple Puff Omelet on page 63, I have listed 2 large Cortland, Jonathan, or Idared apples. Any of these would be my first choice because of their flavor and texture. However, if these varieties were not available, I would choose another that had similar qualities. In this case, I would choose Granny Smith apples that were very light green, an indication that they were ripe and only mildly tart (as opposed to dark green and very tart) and because they have a firm texture. Failing that choice, I would then look for Golden Delicious apples that were more green than yellow, an indication that they were barely ripe, having a firmer texture and a tarter flavor than when completely yellow and fully ripe. If in doubt, refer to the Popular Orchard Varieties descriptions on page 5 in conjunction with the table of Apple Varieties on page 9.

When a recipe calls for one large apple and yours look small to medium, substitute by the cup according to the table of Apple Equivalents on page 17.

SEASONING WITHOUT SALT

I grew up in a family where high blood pressure was a problem. For many years, salt was eliminated from our meals. This created no great exercise for my mother for the simple reason that the English like to keep their taste buds in shape by experiencing a variety of miniature taste explosions.

Our roast beef and ham sandwiches would be liberally smeared with eye-watering Coleman's mustard. Pungent Madras curry was added to ground beef and onions, chicken, and rabbit stews in such quantity that a pitcher of water was absolutely essential to cool our burning throats.

Thyme, sage, parsley, oregano, and garlic were kitchen staples that found their way into a great many stews and casseroles. Because herbs grew outside the kitchen door or were purchased fresh at the greengrocer's, they held no mystery for a country child. It was the aromatic bounty of the Orient and the West Indies—cinnamon, nutmeg, ginger, and long black vanilla beans—that conjured vivid images of exotic, far-off places.

Apples and spices belong together. At times, I've had to restrain my urges to go hog-wild on these very fragrant powders. However, you may find that I wasn't generous enough with the recipes that follow, so by all means experiment and add an extra pinch here and there. What is intense to one person may be lacking in flavor to the next.

So, although my mother uses salt judiciously today, I do not. Those early years were formative, and salt does not play a role in my cooking. However, you may want to add salt to taste in the savory dishes.

BEVERAGES

During the autumn when I buy fresh-pressed apple juice or cider from my local orchards, I like to drink it chilled and unadulterated. I recoil at the thought of adding bananas, orange juice, or, heaven forbid, beer.

However, after the orchards close in December, I'm obliged to buy pasteurized apple juice from the markets. Then I start to think of apple tea, punch, and, in particular, wassail—the traditional Christmas drink of the English.

Cider does freeze well. If you have space in your freezer you might consider buying extra in the fall to carry you through until the orchards reopen.

ICED APPLE TEA

PREPARATION TIME: 15 MINUTES   YIELD: 4 SERVINGS

4 tea bags (orange pekoe or
  herbal)
4 cups boiling water
1 tablespoon honey (optional)
2 cups chilled apple juice or
  cider
4 lemon slices
4 mint sprigs

1. Place the tea bags in a pitcher and cover with the boiling water.
2. Allow to steep for 5 minutes. Squeeze the teabags and discard.
3. Stir in the honey until dissolved.
4. Stir in the apple juice. Chill (or add a couple of ice cubes to each glass).
5. Pour into 4 tall glasses and drop a slice of lemon and a sprig of mint in each.

APPLE SHAKE

PREPARATION TIME: 3 MINUTES   YIELD: 4 SERVINGS

1 pint (2 cups) vanilla ice cream
1 quart cold apple juice or cider
3 ripe bananas
1 teaspoon ground cinnamon

1. Combine all ingredients and blend until smooth.
2. Chill until serving time or use immediately.

APPLE SMOOTHIE

PREPARATION TIME: 5 MINUTES   YIELD: 2 SERVINGS

2 cups apple sauce
1 cup apple juice or cider
1 cup orange juice
2 tablespoons honey
½ teaspoon ground nutmeg
½ teaspoon ground cinnamon

1. Place all the ingredients in a blender and blend until smooth.
2. Serve immediately or serve chilled.

FRUIT CRUSH

PREPARATION TIME: 30 MINUTES   YIELD: 4–6 SERVINGS

½ cup water
½ cup sugar
1 stick cinnamon
4 whole cloves
1 juice orange
1 cup whole strawberries or
  1 cup melon balls
1 cup seedless grapes
1 large apple (Red Delicious,
  McIntosh)
1 lime
1 quart chilled apple juice or
  cider
1 (7-ounce) bottle club soda,
  chilled

1. Heat the water and sugar in a small saucepan over low heat. Stir until the sugar dissolves—about 1 minute.
2. Add the cinnamon and the cloves.
3. Peel the orange and add the zest to the syrup. Remove from the heat.
4. Cut the orange in half and squeeze the juice into the syrup.
5. Hull the strawberries and slice in half. Place in a punch bowl.
6. Halve the grapes and add to the bowl.
7. Core and thinly slice the apple. Drop it into the bowl.
8. Thinly slice the lime. Add to the bowl.
9. Strain the syrup over the fruit.
10. Pour in the apple juice and club soda. Stir and serve in glasses.

APPLE EGGNOG

PREPARATION TIME: 20 MINUTES   YIELD: APPROXIMATELY 18 SERVINGS

4 eggs, separated
½ cup sugar
1 cup brandy
⅓ cup rum
2 cups apple juice or cider
3 cups heavy cream
½ teaspoon ground nutmeg

1. Place the egg yolks in a large punch bowl and beat until pale yellow.
2. Add the sugar and beat until well mixed.
3. Beat in the brandy and rum, a little at a time; then the apple juice.
4. Continue beating and add the heavy cream. Beat several minutes until the mixture is thick.
5. In a medium-size bowl, beat the egg whites until stiff peaks form. Fold into the cream mixture.
6. Sprinkle the nutmeg over the top. Serve at once.

WASSAIL

PREPARATION TIME: 10 MINUTES   BAKING TIME: 40 MINUTES   YIELD: 4 SERVINGS

4 large apples (McIntosh)
¼ cup brown sugar
¼ cup apple juice or cider
3 (12-ounce) bottles of ale
1 cup sherry
1 cinnamon stick
½ teaspoon ground nutmeg
½ teaspoon ground ginger
Zest (rind) of 1 lemon
2 tablespoons brown sugar

The English serve Wassail (from the Anglo-Saxon Wes hal, or "Be whole," a salutation offered when presenting a cup of wine to a guest) or "lambs wool" as it is also known, on Twelfth Night.

1. Preheat the oven to 350°F.
2. Slit the skins of the apples horizontally about halfway around. Place in a greased baking dish and sprinkle with the brown sugar and apple juice. Bake for about 40 minutes, basting frequently. Remove when soft.
3. Pour the rest of the ingredients in a saucepan and simmer for 5 minutes. Add the baked apples, stir thoroughly, and serve hot.

PARTY APPLE PUNCH

PREPARATION TIME: 20 MINUTES   YIELD: 10 SERVINGS

1 small pineapple or 2 (8-ounce) cans unsweetened pineapple chunks or rings
2 apples (Red Delicious)
2 cups apple juice
3 cups sparkling cider or sparkling white wine
1 cup pineapple juice
½ cup brandy, applejack, or vodka

1. Slice the pineapple into ½-inch rings. Remove the peel and roughly chop. Place in a large pan. If you are using canned pineapple, drain the juice and reserve 1 cup for step 2.
2. Core and cut the apples into ¼-inch slices. Add to the pan with the apple juice, sparkling cider or wine, and pineapple juice.
3. Heat for 5–10 minutes, until steaming.
4. Remove from the heat and stir in the liquor.
5. Cool slightly and pour into a punch bowl or pitcher. Serve warm or cold, with or without the fruit.

APPETIZERS AND SNACKS

"An apple a day keeps the doctor away," so the old saying goes. If that's the case, you can feel healthy and self-righteous whenever you snack on an apple. Apples are not greasy, they contain trace vitamins, they are low in sodium and calories, and they freshen and cleanse the mouth.

If an apple out of hand is not exactly what you had in mind, substitute a slice for crackers or bread and spread with some of the delicious concoctions that follow. Or cut an apple into wedges and try them with your favorite dip.

OPEN FACE APPLE SANDWICHES

Forget the bread, crackers, and cookies—substitute apple rings instead. Topped with a variety of spreads, cheeses, and meats, they bring a welcome change to the hors d'oeuvre platter. They are particularly successful with children and weight-conscious adults.

Wash and core the apples and cut into ¼-inch to ½-inch slices. Depending on whether you are making snacks, lunch, or hors d'oeuvres, choose from the following toppings:

- Peanut butter and banana slices
- Peanut butter with raisins
- Peanut butter and apple sauce (or apple butter) in a ratio of 2 parts peanut butter to 1 part apple sauce
- Peanut butter and crumbled bacon
- Peanut butter and chopped dates or chopped nuts
- 8 ounces softened cream cheese mixed with 1 small grated apple, ¼ cup chopped dates, ¼ cup chopped walnuts, and 2 tablespoons honey
- Cream cheese with raisins and chopped nuts
- Cream cheese with onion slices and smoked salmon (or sardines)
- Cream cheese with chopped fresh chives
- Cream cheese and chutney
- Cream cheese, cinnamon, and honey
- Cream cheese with diced ham (or bologna), curry powder, and chutney
- Liverwurst
- Refried beans or mashed baked beans
- Mashed blue cheese
- Canned corned beef with a slice of pickle
- Mozzarella, cheddar, or muenster cheese topped with a slice of tomato and popped under the broiler for 1 minute for mini apple-slice pizzas

APPLE CHEESE SPREAD

PREPARATION TIME: 15 MINUTES, PLUS 1 HOUR CHILLING   YIELD: 2½ CUPS

8 ounces cream cheese at room temperature
1 cup grated cheddar cheese at room temperature
2 tablespoons brandy or sherry
1 medium-size apple (Granny Smith)
¼ teaspoon ground black pepper
1 teaspoon dried thyme
1 teaspoon dried basil
1 teaspoon dried oregano

1. Combine the cream cheese, cheddar cheese, and brandy. Beat until smooth.
2. Peel, core, and grate the apple into the bowl.
3. Sprinkle with the pepper and herbs. Stir until thoroughly combined.
4. Spoon into a covered crock and chill for approximately 1 hour. Serve on toast or crackers.

PROSCUITTO APPLE WEDGES

PREPARATION TIME: 20 MINUTES   YIELD: 32 WEDGES

4 medium-size apples (Red Delicious, Cortland, Empire, Idared)
¼ cup lemon juice
4 ounces cream cheese, softened
½ pound proscuitto or smoked salmon

1. Slice each apple into 8 wedges.
2. Dip each cut surface in lemon juice.
3. Spread the softened cream cheese thinly on each cut side.
4. Wrap each wedge with a thin slice of proscuitto. Refrigerate.
5. Remove from refrigerator 30 minutes before serving.

HOT FRUIT

PREPARATION TIME: 20 MINUTES   YIELD: 2 SERVINGS

1 large grapefruit, peeled and
the skin removed from each
segment or 1 (10-ounce or
thereabouts) can of grapefruit
segments
1 apple (Granny Smith, Golden
Delicious)
1 banana
2 tablespoons raisins
¼ cup apple juice or cider
1 tablespoon honey

This makes a great snack or breakfast on a cold day.

1. Place the grapefruit segments in a medium-size saucepan. (If you are using canned grapefruit, save the juice for another recipe or a drink.)
2. Core and chop the apple. Add to the grapefruit.
3. Peel the banana and slice into ½-inch slices. Mix with the fruit.
4. Add the raisins, apple juice, and honey to the pan and warm over low heat—about 10 minutes. The mixture should be hot enough to eat without scalding the mouth.

APPLE-RAISIN YOGURT

PREPARATION TIME: 10 MINUTES   YIELD: 1 OR 2 SERVINGS

1 small sweet apple (Delicious,
Macoun, McIntosh)
¼ cup granola
2 tablespoons raisins
1 cup yogurt (plain, vanilla, and
lemon are good choices)

This makes a great snack, breakfast, or dessert.

1. Core the apple. Grate into a small bowl.
2. Add the rest of the ingredients and mix together. Chill if desired.

APPLE AND SAUSAGE BUNDLES

PREPARATION TIME: 25 MINUTES, PLUS 4 HOURS MARINATING   COOKING TIME: 6–9 MINUTES
YIELD: APPROXIMATELY 24 PIECES

2 tablespoons soy sauce
½ cup apple juice or cider
½ teaspoon ground cinnamon
½ teaspoon ground ginger
2 tablespoons creamy peanut
    butter
4 veal sausages (Bockwurst),
    about 6 inches long
2 medium-size apples (McIntosh,
    Golden Delicious)
½ pound bacon

1. Blend the soy sauce, apple juice, cinnamon, ginger, and peanut butter together. Pour into a medium-size bowl.
2. Cut the sausages into 1-inch pieces, stir into the peanut butter mixture, cover the bowl, and refrigerate. Marinate for about 4 hours.
3. Core and cut the apples into the same number of slices as there are sausage pieces. (The slices should not be too thin, though.)
4. Drain the sausage pieces and reserve the marinade.
5. Cut the bacon strips in half crosswise and wrap one piece around a slice of apple and a piece of sausage. Secure the bundles with wooden toothpicks. Drop each bundle into the bowl to coat with the marinade.
6. Place the bacon bundles on a broiler rack and broil 4 inches from the heat. Broil them approximately 3 minutes a side, turning them over until the bacon is cooked and crispy.

APPLE
SALADS

The crisp, crunchy, tart, sweet flesh of apples can be diced, sliced, or grated and added to just about any salad you may think of making. The understated flavor of apples lends itself to sweet and sour, creamy, garlic, herbed, and spiced dressings. So when you're short on lettuce, carrots, beets, celery, or any other salad ingredient, slice an apple into your bowl. Add a handful of chopped nuts and some diced, cooked meat, and you'll have a satisfying main course salad.

BANANA-APPLE SALAD

PREPARATION TIME: 15 MINUTES   YIELD: 4–6 SERVINGS

2 large apples (Empire, Idared,
 Jonathan, Red Delicious)
2 tablespoons lemon juice
2 tablespoons water
2 medium-size bananas
1 cup pitted dates (not sugared)
¼ cup chopped walnuts
1 cup vanilla yogurt
2 tablespoons honey

1. Core and dice the apples. Place in a large bowl and sprinkle with the lemon juice and water. Toss.
2. Slice the bananas and chop the dates.
3. Drain the juice from the apples and add the banana slices, dates, and walnuts to the bowl.
4. Beat together the yogurt and honey. Mix with the fruit. Serve chilled.

POTATO APPLE SALAD

PREPARATION TIME: 35 MINUTES   YIELD: 4–6 SERVINGS

6 medium-size potatoes
¼ pound bacon
1 medium-size onion
½ cup vegetable oil
2 tablespoons cider vinegar
1 garlic clove, crushed
2 medium-size apples (Cortland,
 Granny Smith, Delicious)
½ cup mayonnaise
1 tablespoon prepared mustard

1. Place the potatoes in a saucepan, cover with water, put on the lid, and cook for approximately 20 minutes. They should be tender but not falling apart. Peel while still warm and cut into ½-inch slices.
2. While the potatoes are cooking, fry the bacon, drain, and cut into ½-inch pieces. Reserve.
3. Grate the onion into a large bowl.
4. Beat together the oil, vinegar, and garlic in a small bowl.
5. Add the sliced potatoes to the grated onion and, while still warm, toss with the dressing.
6. Core and dice the apples. Add to the potatoes with the bacon.
7. Mix the mayonnaise and mustard and spoon into the bowl. Toss to combine the mixture. Serve warm or chilled.

WALDORF SALAD

PREPARATION TIME: 20 MINUTES   YIELD: 4 SERVINGS

3 medium-size apples (Jonagold,
Cortland, Northern Spy,
Granny Smith)
3 celery ribs, diced
½ cup chopped walnuts
2 tablespoons lemon juice
½ teaspoon ground white pepper
¾ cup heavy cream
8 mint leaves or 2 tablespoons
fresh chopped parsley
1 head Boston lettuce

1. Begin by chilling a medium-size bowl for beating the cream.
2. Core and dice the apples. Place in a large bowl.
3. Add the celery and walnuts to the apples.
4. Beat the lemon juice, white pepper, and heavy cream together in the chilled bowl.
5. When the cream is thick and stands in soft mounds, stir into the apple mixture.
6. Tear the mint leaves into small pieces and sprinkle on the top. Or sprinkle with chopped parsley.
7. Serve on Boston lettuce leaves.

APPLE SLAW

PREPARATION TIME: 20 MINUTES, PLUS 1 HOUR CHILLING   YIELD: 6 SERVINGS

2 medium-size carrots
1 medium-size red onion
4 cups thinly sliced or shredded
red cabbage
2 large apples (Granny Smith)
⅔ cup mayonnaise
⅔ cup sour cream
¼ cup tomato catsup
1 tablespoon lemon juice
½ teaspoon ground black pepper
1 head Boston lettuce

1. Coarsely grate the carrots and onion into a large bowl. Add the cabbage.
2. Core and thinly slice the apples. Add to the cabbage mixture.
3. Beat the mayonnaise, sour cream, catsup, lemon juice, and pepper. Mix into the slaw. Refrigerate for at least 1 hour.
4. Line a large bowl with the Boston lettuce leaves and fill with the chilled apple slaw. Serve immediately.

HELEN BUSCH'S MOLDED APPLE SALAD

1 (3-ounce) package lime or
  lemon-flavored gelatin
1 cup boiling water
1 (16-ounce) can grapefruit or
  mandarin orange sections
2 large apples (Golden Delicious)
½ cup chopped walnuts or
  pecans

1. In a medium-size bowl, dissolve the gelatin in the boiling water.
2. Stir in the fruit sections plus the juice.
3. Peel, core, and thinly slice the apples. Add to the gelatin with the nuts.
4. Rinse 8 individual jello molds or a large mold in cold water. Pour in the gelatin mixture. Chill until firm.

STUFFED APPLE SALAD

4 large apples (Cortland, Red
  Delicious, Mutsu)
½ lemon
2 medium-size tender celery
  ribs, chopped
1 scallion, including green top,
  chopped
2 medium-size carrots, grated
¼ cup chopped walnuts
¼ cup mayonnaise
2 tablespoons sour cream
½ teaspoon ground nutmeg
⅛ teaspoon white pepper
1 head Boston lettuce
1 cup green seedless grapes
  (optional)

1. Core the apples. With a small paring knife, slice off the top and remove the flesh, leaving ¼–½-inch of flesh on the bottom and sides. Rub the tops with the lemon half. Trim the blossom ends to make the apples sit level. Refrigerate.
2. Chop the removed apple flesh and place in a medium-size bowl. Toss with juice squeezed from the lemon half.
3. Add the celery, scallion, carrots, walnuts, mayonnaise, sour cream, nutmeg, and white pepper. Mix well. Refrigerate.
4. Arrange the nicest Boston lettuce leaves on 4 plates. Place the hollowed apples in the middle and fill with the chopped mixture. Sprinkle the grapes all around. Serve at once.

SPINACH APPLE SALAD

PREPARATION TIME: 20 MINUTES   YIELD: 4 SERVINGS

4 cups fresh spinach leaves
1 small head Boston or Bibb
   lettuce
2 medium-size apples (Cortland,
   Granny Smith)
¼ cup chopped walnuts
½ cup plain yogurt
1 tablespoon honey
⅛ teaspoon ground turmeric
⅛ teaspoon ground ginger
⅛ teaspoon ground coriander

1. Place the spinach and lettuce in a salad bowl.
2. Core and slice the apples. Add to the lettuce with the walnuts.
3. Blend together the yogurt, honey, and spices. Toss with the salad. Serve immediately.

CURRIED CHICKEN SALAD

PREPARATION TIME: 20 MINUTES   YIELD: 4–6 SERVINGS

⅔ cup sour cream
⅓ cup mayonnaise
1 tablespoon honey
1 tablespoon lime juice
1 large garlic clove, crushed
1½ teaspoons curry powder
½ teaspoon ground ginger
½ teaspoon ground cumin
2 apples (Granny Smith,
   Northern Spy, Winesap)
2 celery ribs, diced
4 cups skinned, boned, and
   cubed cooked chicken
½ cup golden raisins
1 head Boston lettuce

1. In a medium-size bowl, beat together the sour cream, mayonnaise, honey, and lime juice.
2. Add the garlic, curry, ginger, and cumin to the dressing. Stir until thoroughly combined.
3. Core and dice the apples. Add to the mayonnaise along with the celery, chicken, and raisins.
4. Serve chilled on lettuce.

APPLE
SIDE DISHES

Botanically speaking, the apple is a fruit. However, the characteristic hard, tart flesh of some varieties (and the taste of underripe apples) allows it to take its place among the vegetables.

Try baked, skinned, and mashed apples with creamed potatoes, turnips, carrots, and parsnips. Slice and sauté apples in butter with onions (sauté the onions for 5–10 minutes first). Dice and steam to crunchy tender and toss with brussels sprouts, butter, and nutmeg. Treat apples as a vegetable, and there are many ways to use them.

Among my favorite apple side dishes are apple-based stuffings for poultry. One apple can be added to any stuffing recipe without throwing it off balance. Slice, chop, or grate the apple and sauté with the onions first, or simply combine it in its raw state.

The apple will not impart much flavor, unless it is a particularly tart one, but it will make the stuffing a little moister. Instead of using water, try adding ¼ cup of apple juice to your stuffing—it will make the dressing a touch sweeter. There are stuffing recipes on pages 45–46.

APPLE-ONION PUREE

PREPARATION TIME: 15 MINUTES   COOKING TIME: 30 MINUTES   YIELD: 4 SERVINGS

5 tablespoons sweet butter
1 tablespoon olive oil
2 large red onions, sliced
2 large apples (Winesap,
    Northern Spy, Idared, Golden
    Delicious)
1 tablespoon brown sugar
¼ teaspoon ground black pepper

This is particularly good with roast pork and goose.

1. Heat the butter and olive oil in a large skillet, and add the onions. Sauté for 5 minutes.
2. Peel, core, and slice the apples. Add to the onions and sprinkle with the sugar and pepper.
3. Cover the skillet and cook over low heat for approximately 20 minutes.
4. Remove the lid and cook for 10 minutes, or until the onions are tender and most of the liquid has evaporated.
5. Pour the mixture into a blender or a food processor. Process until the mixture is coarsely blended. Reheat in the skillet and serve.

APPLE AND SWEET POTATO PUREE

PREPARATION TIME: 25 MINUTES   BAKING TIME: 1½ HOURS   YIELD: 6 SERVINGS

2 large sweet potatoes
2 large apples (Rome Beauty,
    Northern Spy, Winesap)
½ cup sweet butter
¼–½ cup heavy or sour cream
½ teaspoon ground nutmeg
¼ teaspoon ground ginger

I like to serve this with roast duck or turkey.

1. Preheat the oven to 350°F.
2. Place the potatoes on a greased baking sheet and bake for 1½ hours, or until very tender.
3. Peel, core, and slice the apples.
4. Melt the butter in a skillet and cook the apples over low heat until tender, about 15 minutes.
5. Skin the potatoes while still hot. Place in a bowl with the cooked apple slices. Add the cream and spices. Mash together with a fork, and then whip the mixture with electric beaters until the texture is creamy. Serve at once.

MAPLE SWEET POTATO CASSEROLE

PREPARATION TIME: 30 MINUTES   BAKING TIME: 30 MINUTES   YIELD: 8–10 SERVINGS

6 medium-size sweet potatoes
2 medium-size apples (Baldwin,
   Granny Smith, Northern Spy)
1 lemon
½ cup sweet butter
½ teaspoon ground nutmeg
½ cup maple syrup

1. Scrub the potatoes and place in a pot of boiling water. Cook for 20 minutes, until they can be easily pierced with a fork. Cool and peel.
2. Preheat the oven to 350°F.
3. Slice the potatoes into ½-inch rings. Arrange a single layer of potatoes in a greased 9-inch by 13-inch baking pan.
4. Peel, core, and slice the apples about ½-inch thick. Toss with the juice of the lemon.
5. Place a single layer of apples over the potatoes. Continue layering until all the apple and potato slices have been used.
6. Melt the butter in a small saucepan, stir in the nutmeg and maple syrup. Pour over the layers.
7. Place in the oven and bake for 30 minutes. Serve hot.

APPLE RATATOUILLE

PREPARATION TIME: 25 MINUTES   COOKING TIME: 50 MINUTES   YIELD: 8 SERVINGS

3 tablespoons olive oil
1 large onion, sliced
4 garlic cloves
2 teaspoons dried basil
1 teaspoon dried oregano
½ teaspoon ground allspice
¼ teaspoon ground black pepper
2 bell peppers, sliced
2 medium-size zucchini, sliced
6 ripe tomatoes, quartered
2 medium-size apples (Rome
   Beauty, Granny Smith,
   Northern Spy), diced

1. Heat the olive oil in a large skillet and add the onion. Crush the garlic directly into the skillet and sauté for 5 minutes.
2. Into the skillet, sprinkle the basil, oregano, allspice, and black pepper.
3. Stir the bell peppers into the onions, and sauté for 10 minutes.
4. Add the zucchini and the tomatoes to the skillet. Stir, cover, and simmer for 20 minutes.
5. Add the apples to the ratatouille, cover, and simmer for 15 minutes. Serve hot.

CHESTNUT-APPLE PUREE

8 ounces fresh chestnuts
2 cups unsweetened apple sauce
½ teaspoon ground nutmeg
¼ teaspoon ground white pepper

This makes a change from the regular apple sauce that accompanies roast pork, game, or goose.

1. Preheat the oven to 400°F.
2. Cut a cross (X) into the flat side of the chestnuts. Place in a shallow baking pan and bake for 15 minutes. Stir occasionally.
3. Remove the chestnuts from the oven and allow to cool slightly. Peel while still warm; otherwise, the brown inner skins are difficult to remove.
4. Pass the peeled chestnuts through a ricer or use a blender or a food processor to puree them. There will be approximately 1½ cups.
5. Place in a 1½-quart baking dish and beat in the apple sauce, nutmeg, and pepper.
6. Keep warm in a low oven until ready to serve.

UNCOOKED CRANBERRY-APPLE RELISH

2 apples (Granny Smith)
1 juice orange
½ cup sugar
2 cups cranberries
1 small onion
2 tablespoons lemon juice
¼ teaspoon cayenne
¼ teaspoon ground cloves
1 teaspoon ground ginger
1 tablespoon brandy

1. Core and cut the apples into about 8 pieces. Process until coarsely chopped in a food processor. Remove to a medium-size bowl.
2. Remove the orange peel in thin strips, being careful not to include the white pith. Process the peel with the sugar in a food processor until finely chopped. Remove to the bowl.
3. Process the cranberries, 1 cup at a time, until coarsely chopped. Add to the apples and orange rind. Squeeze in the orange juice.
4. Peel and cut the onion into 4 pieces. Process until coarsely chopped. Add with the rest of the ingredients to the bowl and stir together.
5. Cover the bowl and refrigerate for a day or two before serving.

RICE-STUFFED APPLES

PREPARATION TIME: 40 MINUTES   BAKING TIME: 45 MINUTES   YIELD: 4 SERVINGS

2 tablespoons sweet butter or
  margarine
1 medium-size onion, chopped
½ cup uncooked rice
1¼ cups water
½ teaspoon ground allspice
½ teaspoon ground ginger
½ cup raisins
4 large apples (Rome Beauty,
  Mutsu, Winesap)
¼ cup apple juice or cider

1. Preheat the oven to 350°F.
2. Heat the butter in a medium-size skillet. Add the onion and sauté for 5 minutes.
3. Stir in the rice, water, allspice, and ginger. Bring to a boil, reduce the heat, and cover the skillet. Simmer for 20 minutes or until the rice is tender, but not soft.
4. Stir in the raisins.
5. Core the apples, leaving about ¼-inch flesh at each bottom. Scoop out approximately ¼-inch flesh from the centers. Chop and add to the rice mixture.
6. Place the apples in a baking dish and spoon the rice stuffing into and on top of the apples. Add the apple juice to the pan.
7. Cut the remaining tablespoon of butter into small pieces and dot over the rice mixture. Cover the pan loosely with aluminum foil.
8. Bake for 45 minutes. Serve hot as a side dish with roast chicken or pork.

APPLE KABOBS

PREPARATION TIME: 15 MINUTES   COOKING TIME: 4 MINUTES   YIELD: 6 SERVINGS

6 medium-size apples
¼ cup sweet butter
½ teaspoon ground cinnamon
½ teaspoon ground nutmeg
½ teaspoon ground ginger
1 tablespoon smooth peanut
  butter

These taste delicious served with ham or chicken.

1. Core and cut the apples into 6 wedges. Cut each wedge in half. Thread on 6 skewers and place on a broiling pan.
2. Melt the butter and stir in the spices and peanut butter.
3. Brush the apple chunks with the mixture and broil for 4 minutes, basting generously each time the skewers are given a quarter turn. Serve hot.

44

APPLE AND RED PEPPER STUFFING BALLS

PREPARATION TIME: 35 MINUTES   BAKING TIME: 45 MINUTES   YIELD: 4 SERVINGS

1 medium-size apple (Granny
   Smith)
1 medium-size onion, chopped
1 garlic clove, minced
2 red bell peppers, chopped
¼ cup sweet butter or margarine
6 slices whole wheat bread
1 teaspoon dried thyme
½ teaspoon ground mace
¼ teaspoon ground black pepper
¼ cup apple juice or cider
1 large egg

1. Core and chop the apple.
2. Melt the butter in a large skillet, and sauté the apple, onion, garlic, and peppers for 10 minutes. Remove from the heat.
3. Cube the bread and add to the skillet with the thyme, mace, black pepper, and apple juice.
4. Beat the egg and stir into the stuffing.
5. Form the stuffing into 4 balls and arrange around a pork or poultry roast for the last 45 minutes or so of roasting time.

SAUSAGE AND APPLE STUFFING

PREPARATION TIME: 15 MINUTES   YIELD: 10 SERVINGS

½ pound pork sausage
1 medium-size apple (Idared,
   Empire, Golden Delicious)
2 medium-size onions, chopped
½ teaspoon dried sage
½ teaspoon dried thyme
½ teaspoon ground ginger
½ teaspoon ground mace
¼ teaspoon ground black pepper
8 slices whole wheat bread
1 large egg

1. Cook the sausage meat in a large skillet for 5 minutes, turning occasionally.
2. Peel, core, and chop the apple. Add the apple and onions to the meat with the spices. Sauté for 5 minutes.
3. Crumble the bread into the pan, beat the egg, and mix all together.
4. Stuff into a 10–12-pound turkey and bake. The stuffing can be baked separately in a greased 1-quart baking dish for 45 minutes at 350°F.

CORN BREAD APPLE STUFFING

PREPARATION TIME: 25 MINUTES   YIELD: STUFFING FOR A 5–6-POUND CHICKEN

1¼ cup sweet butter or margarine
1 medium-size onion, chopped
2 medium-size celery ribs, chopped
¼ cup chopped fresh parsley
1 teaspoon dried oregano
2 medium-size apples (Empire, Idared, Golden Delicious)
2 cups crumbled corn bread (2 large muffins or 4 slices of bread)
2 tablespoons apple juice
1 large egg

1. Heat the butter in a skillet and sauté the chopped vegetables for 5 minutes. Add the parsley and oregano.
2. Peel, core, and chop the apples. Sauté with the onion mixture for 5 minutes.
3. Stir in the corn bread.
4. Beat together the apple juice and the egg. Mix into the stuffing.
5. Stuff into a 5–6-pound chicken and bake. The stuffing can be baked separately in a greased 1½-quart baking dish for 45 minutes at 350°F.

MARLA RATHBUN'S ONION-APPLE STUFFING

PREPARATION TIME: 3½ HOURS   YIELD: STUFFING FOR TWO 6–8-POUND GEESE OR ONE 12–14-POUND TURKEY

½ cup sweet butter or margarine
18 medium-size onions, sliced
5 celery ribs, sliced
½ cup sweet butter
4 cups bread cubes (8 slices of bread)
¼ cup chopped fresh parsley
1 tablespoon chopped fresh sage
1 tablespoon fresh thyme
½ teaspoon freshly ground black pepper
4 large apples (Idared)

1. In a large skillet, melt ½ cup butter. Add the onions and slowly cook for 3 hours. Add more butter if necessary.
2. In a second skillet, melt another ½ cup butter and sauté the celery for 5 minutes.
3. Toss in the bread cubes, herbs, and black pepper.
4. Peel, core, and dice the apples. Mix with the other ingredients.
5. When the onions are a rich brown, stir into the stuffing. Stuff into two 6–8-pound geese or one 12–14-pound turkey. Excess stuffing can be baked separately in a 1½-quart greased baking dish for 45 minutes at 350°F.

APPLES
FOR DINNER

Apple sauce in meatloaf. Of course, it makes a very moist and tasty one. Grated, sliced, or cubed apples add another dimension to savory soups, meat pies, and poultry. They go equally well with pork, beef, and lamb. In fact, is there any meat dish that can't take apples? Whether you are preparing a casual supper or a formal dinner, apples belong on the menu. Here are a few recipes to get your imagination rolling.

MULLIGATAWNY SOUP

PREPARATION TIME: 30 MINUTES   COOKING TIME: 30 MINUTES   YIELD: 4–6 SERVINGS

¼ cup sweet butter or margarine
1 medium-size onion, chopped
1 medium-size carrot, chopped
1 small celery rib, chopped
1 medium-size apple (Granny
   Smith, Newtown Pippin,
   Northern Spy, Stayman)
2 tablespoons all-purpose flour
3 teaspoons curry powder
5 cups chicken stock
1 cup cooked rice
½ cup heavy cream

1. Melt the butter in a 3-quart saucepan, and sauté the onion, carrot, and celery for 5 minutes.
2. Peel, core, and dice the apple. Stir into the vegetables and sauté for 5 minutes.
3. Stir in the flour and curry powder.
4. Gradually pour in the stock and bring to a boil. Reduce the heat, cover the pan, and simmer for 20 minutes.
5. Add the rice and continue simmering for 10 minutes more. Remove from the heat.
6. Pour the heavy cream into a small saucepan and scald. Add to the soup and serve.

ZUCCHINI AND APPLE SOUP

PREPARATION TIME: 15 MINUTES   COOKING TIME: 30–45 MINUTES   YIELD: 4–6 SERVINGS

1 large apple (Rome Beauty,
   Northern Spy, Winesap)
2 tablespoons vegetable oil
2 tablespoons sweet butter
1 large onion, sliced
2 medium-size zucchini, chopped
2 tablespoons vegetable oil
½ cup cider or sherry
½ teaspoon ground black pepper
½ teaspoon ground nutmeg
4 cups chicken stock
½ cup heavy cream
½ cup chopped fresh parsley

1. Peel, core, and dice the apple.
2. Heat the oil and butter in a large skillet, add the vegetables and apples, and sauté over medium heat for 5–10 minutes, until soft.
3. Add the cider or sherry, the pepper, and nutmeg. Cover the pan and simmer for 15 minutes.
4. Add the stock, cover the pan, and simmer for 5 minutes.
5. Puree the vegetables in a blender or food processor (or force through a sieve).
6. Return to the skillet, add the heavy cream, and bring to a fast boil.
7. Pour into serving bowls and sprinkle with chopped parsley, freshly ground pepper, and a little ground nutmeg.

BLACK BEAN SOUP

PREPARATION TIME: 1 HOUR TO PRESOAK THE BEANS, PLUS 15 MINUTES ACTUAL PREPARATION
COOKING TIME: 2–4 HOURS   YIELD: 6–8 SERVINGS

1 pound dried black beans
  (turtle beans)
6 cups water
2 tablespoons olive oil
1 large onion, chopped
4 large garlic cloves, chopped
2 large celery ribs, chopped
2 teaspoons ground allspice
½ cup sherry
3½ cups beef or chicken stock
1 bay leaf
2 tart apples (Granny Smith)
1 pound sweet and spicy Italian
  sausage, sliced in 2-inch pieces

1. Wash and pick over the beans. Place in a large pot, add the water, and heat to boiling. Remove from the heat, cover the pot, and set aside to soak for 1 hour.
2. Heat the olive oil in a 4–5-quart Dutch oven, and sauté the onions, garlic, and celery for 5 minutes.
3. Add the allspice, sherry, stock, and bay leaf. Drain the beans and add to the Dutch oven. Bring to a boil, reduce the heat, and simmer for 2–4 hours (depending on how tender you like the beans).
4. Peel, core, and dice the apples. Add with the sausages to the beans during the last 30 minutes of cooking.
5. Serve over rice.

TUNA-APPLE PITA POCKETS

PREPARATION TIME: 15 MINUTES   YIELD: 4 SERVINGS

1 small apple
1 small celery rib, sliced
1 teaspoon lemon juice
1 small onion, chopped
1 (7-ounce) can tuna
1 teaspoon dried dill weed
½ cup mayonnaise
4 small pita pockets
4 large Boston lettuce leaves

1. Core and chop the apple into a medium-size bowl.
2. Add the celery and sprinkle with lemon juice.
3. Add the onion.
4. Drain the tuna and add to the bowl with the dill and the mayonnaise. Mix well.
5. Cut the top off each pita bread and place a lettuce leaf in each.
6. Stuff with the tuna mixture. Serve.

CHICKEN WITH SOUR CREAM

2 tablespoons vegetable oil

1 large onion, chopped

2–4 garlic cloves, minced

2 medium-size celery ribs, chopped

4-pound chicken, cut into serving pieces

1 teaspoon ground cumin

½ teaspoon ground ginger

½ teaspoon ground cinnamon

¼ teaspoon freshly ground black pepper

1 cup white wine or chicken stock

1 cup tomato juice

2 tablespoons cornstarch

1 tablespoon honey

2 apples (Golden Delicious)

1 cup sour cream at room temperature

1. Preheat the oven to 350°F.
2. Heat the oil in a 5–6-quart Dutch oven, and sauté the onion, garlic, and celery over medium heat.
3. Remove the skin from the chicken and lay the pieces on top of the sautéed vegetables in the Dutch oven. Add the giblets and liver if desired.
4. Sprinkle with the spices.
5. Cover with the wine and tomato juice, reserving a little of the liquid to mix with the cornstarch. Make a paste with the cornstarch and reserved liquid.
6. Bring the liquids in the Dutch oven to a boil, reduce the heat to low, and stir in the cornstarch paste and the honey.
7. Cover the pot and place in the oven for 45 minutes, or until the chicken is nearly tender.
8. Peel, core, and cube the apples. Stir into the pot with the sour cream. Cook 15–20 minutes longer. Serve at once.

APPLE RAREBIT SUPPER

PREPARATION TIME: 25 MINUTES   YIELD: 4 SERVINGS

¾ pound cheddar cheese
1 tablespoon sweet butter or
  margarine
1 large apple (Rome Beauty,
  Winesap)
1 teaspoon dry mustard
½ teaspoon ground nutmeg
½ cup heavy cream
4 slices toasted bread

1. Grate the cheese into a medium-size saucepan. Add the butter.
2. Grate the apple into the pan. Add the mustard, nutmeg, and cream.
3. Heat on low and stir until all the ingredients are blended.
4. When the mixture begins to bubble, pour over buttered toast, and serve.

BAKED APPLES AND CHEESE

PREPARATION TIME: 15 MINUTES   BAKING TIME: 40–45 MINUTES   YIELD: 6 SERVINGS

1 large leek
2 tablespoons sweet butter or
  margarine
3 cups canned apple slices (page
  134), drained
1 cup grated cheddar cheese
1½ cups half-and-half or light
  cream
3 large eggs
1 teaspoon ground nutmeg
¼ teaspoon freshly ground black
  pepper

1. Preheat the oven to 350°F.
2. Wash the leek and discard the outer layer and any of the tougher green leaves. Slice into ¼-inch rings.
3. Heat the butter in a skillet, and add the leek. Sauté for 5 minutes. Turn into an 8-inch by 8-inch baking dish.
4. Layer the apple slices on top and sprinkle with the grated cheese.
5. Beat the cream, eggs, nutmeg, and pepper. Pour over the cheese.
6. Place the dish in the oven and bake for 40–45 minutes, until the custard is set and a knife inserted in the center comes out clean.
7. Serve hot, warm, or cold, as a light main dish or for brunch.

CIDER-BRAISED CHICKEN

PREPARATION TIME: 15 MINUTES   COOKING TIME: 60 MINUTES   YIELD: 4 SERVINGS

4-pound chicken, cut in quarters
1 tablespoon ground turmeric
1 teaspoon ground ginger
½ teaspoon ground mace
¼ teaspoon ground allspice
4 tomatoes, quartered
1 cup apple juice or cider
1 tablespoon cornstarch
2 tablespoons cold water

1. Remove the wing tips, back bone, and parson's nose from the chicken pieces; freeze for stock making. Discard any fat.
2. Brown the chicken in a large skillet over medium heat (do not use oil) skin-side down for about 10 minutes. Pour off the excess fat.
3. Sprinkle with the ground spices and tomatoes. Cover with the apple cider.
4. Cover the pan, reduce the heat, and simmer for 45 minutes.
5. To thicken the juices, make a paste by combining the cornstarch with the cold water. Stir into the juices and simmer uncovered for 15 minutes longer.

COD AND APPLE CURRY

PREPARATION TIME: 25 MINUTES   COOKING TIME: 25 MINUTES   YIELD: 4 SERVINGS

2 tablespoons olive oil
1 large onion, chopped
2 garlic cloves, minced
2 teaspoons curry powder (or to taste)
1 (28-ounce) can crushed tomatoes
2 tablespoons chutney
¼ cup raisins
2 medium-size apples (Golden Delicious, Macoun)
1½ pounds cod steaks

1. Heat the oil in a large skillet and sauté the onion and garlic for 10 minutes.
2. Add the curry powder, tomatoes, chutney, and raisins to the skillet.
3. Peel, core, and chop the apples. Stir into the simmering mixture. Cook for 15–20 minutes, until the vegetables are tender.
4. Remove the skin and bones, if necessary, from the fish steaks, and cut into bite-size pieces. Stir into the curry and cook for 5–10 minutes— just until tender. Serve over rice.

BRAISED DUCK

PREPARATION TIME: ABOUT 1½–1¾ HOURS   BAKING TIME: 1¾ HOURS   YIELD: 4 SERVINGS

5½–6-pound duckling (plus neck,
  gizzard, heart, and liver)
4 cups stock or water
2 garlic cloves, flattened
1 celery rib
1 small onion, halved
1 carrot, cut up
2 garlic cloves, flattened
1 large onion, chopped
2 medium-sized carrots, chopped
2 medium-size celery ribs,
  chopped
2 garlic cloves, minced
1 teaspoon dried thyme
1 teaspoon dried sage
1 teaspoon ground mace
½ teaspoon ground allspice
¼ teaspoon freshly ground black
  pepper
⅛ teaspoon cayenne
1 cup red wine
2 tablespoons cornstarch
3 apples (Granny Smith)

This is a superb company dish that can be prepared two days ahead of time. The advantage of cooking duck in advance is that all the fat can be removed from the juices when the duck is chilled. Because we are all so conscious of removing unnecessary cholesterol and fats from our diets, this is a habit I have adopted whenever I make stews from fatty cuts of meat, such as chuck, pork, oxtail, and chicken with the skin on.

1. Place the neck, gizzard, heart, and liver in a medium-size saucepan and cover with 4 cups stock or water. Add 2 flattened garlic cloves, 1 celery rib, 1 small onion, and 1 carrot. Bring to a boil, reduce the heat, place the lid askew, and simmer for 40 minutes.
2. Cut the duck into serving-size pieces, and remove any fat from around the neck and vent areas. Cut off the wing tips and parson's nose and discard.
3. In a 4-quart or 5-quart Dutch oven, brown the duck pieces, skin-side down (do not use any fat or oil) for 20 minutes to render the fat. Add 2 flattened garlic cloves to the pan during the browning.
4. Remove the duck pieces to a plate. Discard the garlic. Drain off all but 2 tablespoons fat and discard.
5. In the 2 tablespoons fat, sauté the large onion, 2 carrots, 2 celery ribs, and minced garlic. Sprinkle with the thyme, sage, mace, allspice, black pepper, and cayenne. Sauté for 10 minutes.
6. Place the browned duck pieces, skin side up, on top of the vegetables in the Dutch oven.
7. Strain the stock and skim off the fat. (I use one of those fat jugs which allows fats to rise to the top. Or I make the stock a day ahead of time and scrape the solid fat off the chilled liquid.)
8. Preheat the oven to 325°F.
9. Add the red wine to the stock and pour over the duck and vegetables. Cover the pot and roast in the preheated oven for 1¼ hours.

10. At this point, the duck can be refrigerated for a day or two so that any remaining fat can solidify and be scraped off.
11. Preheat the oven to 325°F.
12. Place the Dutch oven on top of the stove and simmer for 15 minutes.
13. Remove the duck pieces to a dish, cover, and keep warm. Place the vegetables and liquid in a blender with the cornstarch. Puree until smooth and return to the Dutch oven with the duck pieces.
14. Peel, core, and cube the apples into ½-inch pieces. Stir into the duck, cover the pot, and return to the oven to bake for 30 minutes, or until the duck is tender.

PORK TENDERLOIN WITH APPLES

PREPARATION TIME: 10 MINUTES   BAKING TIME: 40–45 MINUTES   YIELD: 4 SERVINGS

2-pound pork tenderloin
3 large garlic cloves, minced
1½ tablespoons prepared mustard
1 teaspoon dried rosemary or 1 tablespoon fresh
½ teaspoon ground mace
¼ teaspoon ground cloves
2 tablespoons apple juice or white wine
1 (28-ounce) can crushed tomatoes
3 large apples (Golden Delicious)

1. Preheat the oven to 450°F.
2. Place the tenderloin in a lightly oiled baking dish.
3. Mix the garlic with the mustard, rosemary, mace, and cloves. Spread over the pork.
4. Bake for 10 minutes, baste with the apple juice, and reduce the oven to 400°F. Roast another 10 minutes uncovered.
5. Layer the tomatoes over the top.
6. Peel, core, and cut the apples into ½-inch slices. Add to the tomatoes around the pork. Bake for 20 minutes or until a meat thermometer registers 170°F.

LAMB STEW

PREPARATION TIME: 15–30 MINUTES   COOKING TIME: 2 HOURS   YIELD: 8–10 SERVINGS

2 tablespoons vegetable oil
3 garlic cloves, minced
1-inch cube fresh ginger root,
    minced
1 large onion, diced
2 celery ribs, diced
2 medium-size carrots, diced
½ teaspoon ground cinnamon
¼ teaspoon ground cloves
⅛ teaspoon cayenne
4 pounds lean lamb shoulder,
    cut in 2-inch cubes
3 cups chicken or vegetable stock
1½ cups red wine or flat beer
2–3 tablespoons cornstarch
3 tablespoons cold water
2 large apples (Granny Smith)

1. Heat the oil in a 6-quart Dutch oven and sauté the garlic, ginger, and diced vegetables for 10 minutes. Sprinkle with the spices.
2. Add the lamb and pour in the stock and wine. Cover the pot and simmer for 1½ hours.
3. Mix the cornstarch to a paste in the cold water and stir into the stew to thicken to the desired consistency.
4. Peel, core, and cube the apples, add to the lamb, and simmer for 30 minutes.

POLISH SAUSAGE, APPLES, AND RED CABBAGE

PREPARATION TIME: 25 MINUTES   COOKING TIME: 30–40 MINUTES   YIELD: 4–6 SERVINGS

2 tablespoons vegetable oil
2 medium-size onions, thinly
  sliced
2 garlic cloves, minced
1 medium-size red cabbage,
  shredded
4 apples (Granny Smith)
2½ pounds kielbasa sausage
1 bay leaf
1 teaspoon dried thyme
½ teaspoon ground mace
½ teaspoon freshly ground black
  pepper
½ cup beef, chicken, or vegetable
  stock
1 tablespoon wine vinegar

1. Heat the oil in a 4-quart kettle and sauté the onions and garlic for 5 minutes.
2. Stir the cabbage into the onions and sauté for 5 minutes.
3. Peel, core, and slice the apples and toss into the pot. Stir all together.
4. Place the sausage in the pot with the vegetables. Add the bay leaf, and sprinkle with the thyme, mace, and black pepper.
5. Pour over the stock and vinegar, cover the pot, and bring to the boil. Reduce the heat and simmer for 30–40 minutes.
6. Remove the sausage and cut into serving-size portions. Arrange the vegetables on a warm serving dish with the sausage pieces on top.

BEEF AND APPLE DEEP DISH PIE

PREPARATION TIME: 40 MINUTES   COOKING AND BAKING TIME: 1¾ HOURS   YIELD: 6 SERVINGS

¼ cup all-purpose flour
½ teaspoon ground mace
½ teaspoon ground cinnamon
½ teaspoon ground ginger
1 teaspoon dried thyme
½ teaspoon ground black pepper
2 pounds boneless chuck or
    round stew meat, cut in 1-inch
    chunks
4 tablespoons vegetable oil
2 tablespoons margarine or
    vegetable oil
2 large onions, thinly sliced
2 cups beef stock
1 cup red wine
2 medium-size apples (Granny
    Smith, Baldwin, Rhode Island
    Greening)
Pastry for a single pie crust
    (pages 125–128)

This is a variation on the classic English dish: Pork and Apple Pie.

1. Mix the flour with the mace, cinnamon, ginger, thyme, and black pepper. Dredge the beef chunks in the spiced flour and reserve any flour that is left.
2. Heat 2 tablespoons of the oil in a Dutch oven and sauté half of the beef until browned on all sides. Remove to a plate and repeat with 2 more tablespoons of oil and the rest of the meat.
3. Heat the 2 tablespoons margarine in the Dutch oven and sauté the onions for 5 minutes. Add the rest of spiced flour to the onions and cook for 5 minutes.
4. Add the beef stock and wine and continue cooking over medium heat until the liquid is steaming. Scrape up any browned flour sticking to the sides.
5. Add the browned beef, cover the pot, and simmer over very low heat for 1 hour.
6. During the last 15 minutes, preheat the oven to 400°F. Peel, core, and thinly slice the apples. Roll out the pastry to fit a 2-quart deep casserole.
7. Spoon the cooked beef into the casserole, cover with the sliced apples, and top with the pastry. Seal the edges to the rim with the tines of a fork. Cut a small steam hole in the center. Brush with beaten egg or milk, if desired.
8. Bake for 45 minutes, or until the crust is golden brown.

CURRIED HAM AND APPLES

2 tablespoons margarine
2 tablespoons flour
1 tablespoon mild curry powder
2¼ cups milk
2 medium-size sweet apples
   (Golden Delicious, Mutsu,
   Empire)
½ cup raisins
1-pound thick (about ¾-inch)
   center-cut slice fully cooked
   ham

1. Melt the margarine in a medium-size skillet. Stir in the flour and curry powder and cook for 1 minute.
2. Pour in the milk, and using a wooden spoon or wire whisk, stir to make a smooth sauce.
3. Peel, core, and dice the apples. Add to the curry sauce with the raisins. Cook over low heat for 10 minutes.
4. Cube the ham (remove fat and bone, if necessary) and stir into the pan. Cook for 10 minutes or until heated through.

LOUISE SALINGER'S APPLE MEATLOAF

3 small slices fresh bread (1½
   cups fresh bread crumbs)
1 medium-size onion
¼ cup catsup
½ teaspoon seasoned pepper
1½ teaspoons prepared mustard
1 large egg
1 pound ground beef
1 pound ground veal or pork
1 cup apple sauce
3 tablespoons apple cider
1 teaspoon prepared mustard
3 tablespoons brown sugar

Louise and Bob Salinger live right in the middle of their orchard in Brewster, New York. Bob and son Bruce come in for lunch at midday, and Louise likes to serve them something substantial that doesn't take much preparation. This meatloaf is one of their favorites.

1. Preheat the oven to 350°F.
2. Crumble the bread into a large mixing bowl.
3. Grate in the onion. Add the catsup, pepper, mustard, egg, beef, and veal.
4. Mix together and shape into a round loaf. Place in a baking pan and bake for 1 hour.
5. In a small saucepan, heat together the apple sauce, apple cider, 1 teaspoon prepared mustard, and the brown sugar.
6. Pour over the meatloaf and continue baking for 30 minutes.

CURRIED MEATLOAF

PREPARATION TIME: 15 MINUTES, PLUS 5 MINUTES FOR GRAVY   BAKING TIME: 60 MINUTES   YIELD: 6 SERVINGS

2 slices whole wheat bread
1 medium-size onion
1 large tart apple (Granny Smith,
    Twenty Ounce, Rhode Island
    Greening)
½ cup raisins (optional)
½ cup plain yogurt
2 tablespoons steak sauce
1 large egg
2 teaspoons curry powder
1 teaspoon dried thyme
1 pound ground beef
1 pound ground pork

This meat mixture makes delicious meatballs, too. Just shape the meat into 2-inch balls and brown in 1 tablespoon of oil in a small Dutch oven. Drain off the fat, add ½ cup tomato sauce, cover the pan, and bake for 30 minutes.

1. Preheat the oven to 350°F.
2. Crumble the bread slices into a large mixing bowl. Grate in the onion.
3. Peel, core, and finely chop the apple. Add to the bowl.
4. Add the rest of the ingredients and mix well. (I use my hands and squish it together.) Turn into a 9-inch by 5-inch pan, cover, and bake for 1 hour.
5. To make a gravy from the pan juices, pour the juices into a skillet. Mix 1 teaspoon of curry powder and 1 teaspoon cornstarch in 2 tablespoons apple juice until smooth. Add to the pan juices; heat and stir until thickened. To make thicker, use 2 teaspoons of cornstarch; for a thinner gravy, add a little milk.

The griddle, or girdle, is one of our simplest and oldest cooking utensils—centuries ago the Gaels used hot stones called *greadeal*—and it is still used for the traditional baked goods in Britain, France, and the United States.

There are many traditional griddle cakes which vary from region to region. They come in the form of hotcakes, johnnycakes, hoe-cakes, fritters, scones, tea pancakes, bannocks, flapjacks, and crumpets—to list just a few.

Griddle cakes are speedy and easy to make, which makes them a great breakfast favorite. In Europe, though, we also eat them for after-noon tea and supper.

Ideally, the griddle or skillet should be of cast iron or heavy aluminum to allow the cakes to brown without burning as they are baked on a moderately hot burner.

Because eggs also play an important role at breakfast, omelet and scrambled egg recipes are included in this section.

APPLE PUFF OMELET

PREPARATION TIME: 20 MINUTES   BAKING TIME: 8–10 MINUTES   YIELD: 4 SERVINGS

2 large apples (Cortland,
Jonathan, Idared)
¼ cup sweet butter
¼ cup brown sugar
1 teaspoon ground cinnamon
4 large eggs
¼ cup sugar
¼ teaspoon cream of tartar
1 tablespoon confectioners' sugar

1. Preheat the oven to 450°F.
2. Peel, core, and thinly slice the apples.
3. Heat the butter in a medium-size skillet, and sauté the apples for 5 minutes over low heat.
4. Mix together the brown sugar and cinnamon. Sprinkle over the apples. Toss and continue to sauté the apples for about 10 minutes, until they caramelize. The mixture will be thick and syrupy.
5. Spoon the mixture into an 8-inch by 8-inch (or thereabouts) baking dish and keep hot in the oven.
6. Separate the eggs. Whisk the yolks and the granulated sugar in a small bowl until fairly thick.
7. In a large bowl, beat the egg whites with the cream of tartar until stiff and shiny. Fold into the yolk mixture, a third at a time.
8. Pour the egg mixture over the apples and bake for 8-10 minutes. The omelet will be puffed and golden. Remove from the oven and sprinkle with confectioners' sugar. Serve immediately.

APPLE SCRAMBLE

PREPARATION TIME: 15 MINUTES   YIELD: 2 SERVINGS

2 large eggs
1 tablespoon honey
1 medium-size apple (Granny
Smith)
1 teaspoon vegetable oil
1 tablespoon sweet butter

1. Beat the eggs with the honey.
2. Grate the apple into the eggs. Stir to mix.
3. Heat the oil and butter in a skillet. When it starts to sizzle, pour in the eggs.
4. Start stirring immediately with a wooden spoon. Cook for 3 or 4 minutes, or until the eggs are cooked.
5. Serve on buttered toast for breakfast or a hot snack.

APPLE ORANGE OMELET

PREPARATION TIME: 15 MINUTES   YIELD: 2–4 SERVINGS

1½ teaspoons cornstarch
¼ cup apple juice or cider
1 tablespoon honey
1 apple (Golden Delicious)
1 teaspoon grated orange rind
1 tablespoon sweet butter or
  margarine
3 large eggs
1 tablespoon sugar

1. Put the cornstarch in a small saucepan and mix to a thin paste with a drop of the apple juice. Stir in the rest of the juice and the honey. Cook over low heat, stirring all the time, until the mixture is thick and bubbling. Remove from the heat.
2. Peel, core, and thinly slice the apple. Stir into the cornstarch mixture with the grated orange rind. Heat gently for 2 minutes.
3. Melt the butter in a medium-size skillet over medium heat. Lightly beat the eggs and sugar together and add to the foaming butter. Shake the pan to spread the eggs. As they set, use a fork to make a zigzag pattern from the edges to the center in several places. Shake the pan to keep the uncooked egg mixture moving.
4. After 2 minutes, the egg should be set underneath and the top should be creamy. Remove from the heat and spoon most of the warm filling on one side of the eggs.
5. Fold the other half over the filling and slide the omelet onto a warm plate. Spoon the remaining filling on top and to the side of the omelet. Serve immediately.

SAUSAGE AND APPLE OMELET

PREPARATION TIME: 30 MINUTES   YIELD: 2 SERVINGS

4 ounces sausage meat
3 scallions, including the green
  tops, sliced
1 medium-size apple (Granny
  Smith, Baldwin, Rhode Island
  Greening)
1 tablespoon sweet butter or
  margarine
4 large eggs
Freshly ground black pepper

1. In a medium-size skillet, brown the sausage meat, breaking it up and turning it as it cooks, for about 8 minutes. Drain off most of the fat and push the meat to one side.
2. Sauté the scallions for 2 minutes in the sausage skillet.
3. Peel, core, and chop the apple. Stir into the sausage meat and scallions and cook over low heat for 5 minutes. Remove from the heat and cover to keep warm.
4. Heat the butter in a medium-size skillet over medium heat. Lightly beat the eggs and add to the foaming butter. Shake the pan to spread the eggs. As they set, use a fork to make a zigzag pattern from the edges to the center in several places. Shake the pan to keep the uncooked egg mixture moving.
5. After 2–3 minutes, the eggs should be set underneath and the top should be creamy. Remove from the heat and spoon the warm filling onto one side of the eggs.
6. Fold the other half over the filling and slide the omelet onto a warm plate. Serve immediately.

APPLE FRITTATA

PREPARATION TIME: 35 MINUTES   COOKING TIME: 10 MINUTES   YIELD: 2–4 SERVINGS

2 tablespoons vegetable or olive oil
1 medium-size onion, chopped
1 red or green bell pepper, chopped
1 garlic clove, minced
1 medium-size apple (Granny Smith)
4 large eggs
2 tablespoons water
½ teaspoon dried sage
¼ teaspoon ground mace
⅛ teaspoon ground black pepper
½ cup grated cheddar, Jack, or mozzarella cheese

1. Heat the oil in a medium-size skillet. Add the onion, pepper, and garlic, and cook over low heat until the onion is tender, about 15 minutes.
2. Peel, core, and thinly slice the apple. Add to the vegetables and cook for 5 minutes.
3. Beat the eggs with the water, sage, mace, and pepper. Pour over the vegetables. Sprinkle with the grated cheese.
4. Cover the pan and cook over low heat for 10 minutes, until the eggs are set and the cheese has melted. Serve at once.

BREAKFAST SAUSAGE CRÊPES

PREPARATION TIME: 55 MINUTES   YIELD: 4 SERVINGS

2 cups canned apple slices (page 134), drained
½ teaspoon ground mace
½ teaspoon ground cinnamon
3 tablespoons sweet butter or margarine
8 link sausages, 5–6 inches long
8 crêpes (page 124)
Maple syrup

1. Sprinkle the apple slices with the mace and cinnamon.
2. Heat the butter in a medium-size skillet and sauté the apples for about 15 minutes, or until soft and golden. Keep warm.
3. Prick the sausages and cook over low heat in a greased skillet for about 10 minutes. Keep warm in a low oven or covered on top of the stove.
4. Make the crêpes according to the basic recipe.
5. Roll the pancakes around the sausages, top with sautéed apples, and serve hot with maple syrup.

APPLE CHEDDAR CRÊPES

PREPARATION TIME: 60 MINUTES   BAKING TIME: 15 MINUTES   YIELD: 4 SERVINGS

3 cups canned apple slices (page 134), drained
¼ cup apple juice or cider
1 teaspoon ground nutmeg
8 crêpes (page 124)
1 cup grated cheddar or Cheshire cheese
1 tablespoon melted butter

1. Combine the apple slices, juice, and nutmeg in a medium-size skillet, and simmer over low heat for 10–15 minutes, until the apples are tender and the liquid has almost evaporated.
2. Preheat the oven to 375°F. Grease a shallow 9-inch by 13-inch baking dish.
3. Make the crêpes, following the basic recipe on page 124, and fill each one with about ¼ cup of apple mixture topped with 2 tablespoons or so of the grated cheese. (Spoon the filling on the lower third and roll up from the bottom.)
4. Place the crêpes, seam side down, in the greased dish. Brush with a little melted butter and bake for 15 minutes, or until hot.

GRATED APPLE FRITTERS

PREPARATION TIME: 15 MINUTES   COOKING TIME: 2–3 MINUTES PER BATCH   YIELD: 2–4 SERVINGS (12–16 FRITTERS)

1 large apple (Rome Beauty)
2 large eggs
½ cup presifted all-purpose flour
½ teaspoon baking powder
½ teaspoon baking soda
½ teaspoon ground nutmeg
½ teaspoon ground cinnamon
Margarine or vegetable oil for frying

1. Peel, core, and grate the apple into a medium-size bowl.
2. Separate the eggs. Drop the whites into a large bowl, the yolks into a small one. Whisk the yolks until light and stir into the grated apple. Add the flour, baking powder, baking soda, and spices, and stir to combine.
3. Beat the egg whites until stiff and fold into the apple mixture.
4. Heat the margarine or vegetable oil in a hot skillet. There should be at least ¼ inch of cooking fat. Drop the batter by the heaping tablespoon into the hot fat. Cook for about 1 minute, turn, and cook the second side for the same length of time. The fritters should be golden brown. Drain on absorbent paper and serve immediately or keep warm in a low oven.

APPLE PANCAKES

PREPARATION TIME: 10 MINUTES, PLUS 30–60 MINUTES RESTING TIME   COOKING TIME: 15 MINUTES
YIELD: 4–6 SERVINGS (16–20 PANCAKES)

2 cups presifted all-purpose flour
1½ teaspoons baking powder
1 teaspoon baking soda
1 teaspoon ground cinnamon
¼ cup sugar or honey
¼ cup apple juice or cider
¼ cup vegetable oil or melted
  sweet butter
2 cups sour cream (or 1½ cups
  plain yogurt)
2 large eggs
2 medium-size apples (McIntosh,
  Golden Delicious, Empire)
Margarine or shortening for
  frying

This batter can be used for waffles as well as pancakes.

1. Place all the ingredients (except the apples and margarine or shortening) in a large mixing bowl, blender, or food processor. Beat or blend until smooth. The batter will be very thick. Allow the batter to rest for 30–60 minutes.
2. Core and grate the apples. Stir into the batter.
3. Heat a heavy skillet over medium-high heat and grease with approximately 1 teaspoon of margarine. Drop the batter onto the hot griddle a few tablespoons at a time (for larger pancakes measure ¼ cup of batter).
4. When bubbles appear on top after approximately 2 minutes, turn and brown the other side. Serve with butter, lemon juice, and sugar.

GIRDLE SCONES

PREPARATION TIME: 20 MINUTES   BAKING TIME: 9 MINUTES   YIELD: 8 SCONES

¾ cup all-purpose flour
½ teaspoon ground cinnamon
½ teaspoon ground nutmeg
1 teaspoon baking powder
½ teaspoon baking soda
¾ cup whole wheat flour
¼ cup sugar
¼ cup sweet butter or margarine
1 large egg
¼ cup plain yogurt or buttermilk
1 large apple (McIntosh, Golden Delicious)

1. Sift the all-purpose flour, cinnamon, nutmeg, baking powder, and baking soda into a large bowl. Add the whole wheat flour and sugar and mix together.
2. Cut in the butter with a pastry blender until the mixture resembles large crumbs. Make a well in the center.
3. Beat the egg and yogurt together in a small bowl.
4. Peel, core, and finely chop the apple. Stir into the liquids.
5. Pour the yogurt mixture into the center of the dry ingredients and, using a fork, stir to form a soft dough.
6. Using a floured board, pat the dough into a ½-inch thick round and cut into 8 triangles.
7. Heat a "girdle" (as we call the griddle in Britain) or heavy skillet over low to medium heat and sprinkle lightly with flour. Bake the scone triangles for 5 minutes, until they are golden brown underneath. Turn and bake for 4 minutes longer.
8. Serve warm. Split and spread with butter.

APPLE DOUGHNUTS

PREPARATION TIME: 15 MINUTES, PLUS 60 MINUTES RESTING TIME   COOKING TIME: 15 MINUTES
YIELD: 20 DOUGHNUTS

2½ cups presifted all-purpose flour
1½ teaspoons baking powder
1 teaspoon baking soda
½ teaspoon ground cinnamon
3 tablespoons sweet butter or margarine, softened
½ cup sugar
1 large egg
¼ cup milk
¼ cup apple juice or cider
1 tablespoon vanilla extract
1 medium-size apple (McIntosh, Golden Delicious)
2–4 cups vegetable oil for deep frying

1. In a large bowl, combine the flour, baking powder, baking soda, and cinnamon. Make a well in the center.
2. In a small bowl, cream together the butter and sugar. Beat in the egg.
3. Add the milk, apple juice, and vanilla. Beat all together. Pour into the center of the dry ingredients and stir until smooth.
4. Peel, core, and finely chop the apple and stir into the batter.
5. Cover and chill the dough for 1 hour.
6. Place half of the dough on a floured board, knead lightly, and roll out to approximately ⅜ inch thick. Cut with a floured 2½-inch doughnut cutter.
7. Heat the oil to 375°F. in a wok or skillet. Fry the dough for 1–2 minutes on each side until golden brown. Do not overcrowd. Drain on absorbent paper and dust or glaze while warm. To dust the doughnuts, sift 1 cup sifted confectioners' sugar with 1 tablespoon ground cinnamon, and sprinkle over the doughnuts. To make a glaze, stir 2 tablespoons apple juice into the sugar and cinnamon mixture. Brush over the doughnuts.

APPLE FRITTERS

1¼ cups presifted all-purpose flour
1 cup beer
1 tablespoon vegetable oil
1 tablespoon sugar
2 large eggs
5 large apples (Rome Beauty, Mutsu)
2–4 cups vegetable oil for deep frying
¼ cup flour
Confectioners' sugar

These apple ring fritters taste good at any time of the day. Try them for breakfast, snacks, and desserts.

1. Combine the sifted flour, beer, 1 tablespoon vegetable oil, sugar, and egg yolks in a blender or food processor. Whirl until smooth. Cover and leave at room temperature for at least 1 hour.
2. Core and slice the apples into ½-inch rings.
3. Pour at least 2 inches of oil into a wok or large skillet. Heat to 375°F.
4. Beat the egg whites in a large bowl until stiff. Stir the batter and fold in the egg whites.
5. Dip the apple rings first in the ¼ cup flour to coat both sides, then in the batter. Fry a few at a time in the hot oil for 2–3 minutes on each side, until golden brown. Drain on absorbent paper.
6. Sprinkle with confectioners' sugar or serve with Apple-Maple Sauce. To make the sauce, blend 2 cups apple sauce with ⅓ cup maple syrup and 1 teaspoon ground cinnamon or mixed spices. Serve immediately.

APPLE CORN HOTCAKES

PREPARATION TIME: 15 MINUTES   COOKING TIME: 4–5 MINUTES PER BATCH   YIELD: 4–8 SERVINGS (8 HOTCAKES)

1 medium-size apple (Granny Smith)
1 tablespoon sweet butter or margarine
1 scallion, thinly sliced
¾ cup yellow cornmeal
¼ cup presifted all-purpose flour
½ teaspoon baking powder
½ teaspoon baking soda
½ teaspoon ground mace
⅛ teaspoon cayenne
1 large egg
¾ cup milk
½ cup grated cheddar cheese
Margarine or vegetable oil to coat the griddle

Great for breakfast, these tasty, savory hotcakes also can replace bread or a side dish with sausage, pork, or poultry dishes. The hotcakes are quite filling; often one per person will suffice. Leftover hotcakes can be crumbled and used as stuffing for roasted Cornish game hens or chicken.

1. Core and finely chop the apple.
2. Melt the butter in a skillet, and sauté the apple and scallion for 3 minutes.
3. In a large bowl, mix the cornmeal, flour, baking powder, baking soda, mace, and cayenne. Make a well in the center.
4. In a small bowl, beat the egg, milk, and cheese. Add the sautéed apple apple and scallion. Stir into the dry ingredients.
5. Heat approximately 1 teaspoon margarine on a griddle or in a heavy skillet over medium heat. When the margarine is hot, drop ¼ cup of batter on the griddle at a time and cook for 2 minutes or so, until the hotcakes are golden underneath. Turn and cook for 3 minutes more. Serve immediately with butter, or keep warm in the oven.

APPLE QUICK BREADS AND MUFFINS

Dice an apple and throw it into your favorite bread or muffin recipe. Use apple juice for the liquid. The difference in flavor may not knock you out, but you will be getting extra nutrition.

I can't advise being quite so cavalier with apple sauce. Too much will alter the texture and density of your baked goods. So if you plan to experiment, be cautious the first time around.

Cream cheese spreads are delicious on apple quick breads. The spreads can be applied to individual slices or the entire bread can be frosted with the spread. You'll find recipes for some of my favorite spreads at the end of this chapter.

APPLE BANANA BREAD

PREPARATION TIME: 15 MINUTES   BAKING TIME: 60 MINUTES   YIELD: 12–16 SLICES

1¾ cups presifted all-purpose flour
2 teaspoons baking powder
½ teaspoon baking soda
2–3 ripe bananas (to make 1 cup mashed)
½ cup brown sugar
⅓ cup vegetable oil
2 large eggs
1 medium-size apple

1. Preheat the oven to 350°F. Grease and flour an 8-inch by 4-inch loaf pan.
2. In a large mixing bowl, combine the flour, baking powder, and baking soda. Make a well in the center.
3. In a medium-size bowl, mash the bananas. Beat in the sugar, oil, and eggs. Pour into the center of the dry ingredients and stir until just combined.
4. Peel, core, and dice the apple. Fold into the batter.
5. Turn into the prepared loaf pan and bake for about 1 hour, or until a skewer inserted in the center comes out clean. Cool in the pan for 10 minutes. Remove and cool completely on a wire rack.

LOUISE SALINGER'S APPLE TEA BREAD

PREPARATION TIME: 25 MINUTES   BAKING TIME: 60 MINUTES   YIELD: 12–16 SLICES

¼ cup sweet butter or margarine, softened
¾ cup sugar
2 large eggs
2 cups presifted all-purpose flour
1 teaspoon baking powder
1 teaspoon baking soda
2 large apples (Northern Spy, Winesap)
1 tablespoon lemon juice
1 teaspoon grated lemon rind
¾ cup chopped walnuts

1. Preheat the oven to 350°F. Grease and flour an 8-inch by 4-inch loaf pan.
2. Cream the butter and sugar together in a large bowl.
3. Beat in the eggs.
4. Sift in the flour, baking powder, and baking soda. Stir to combine.
5. Core the apples and grate into the mixture.
6. Add the lemon juice, lemon rind, and the chopped walnuts. Mix thoroughly. Pour into the prepared pan.
7. Bake for 1 hour or until a skewer inserted in the center comes out clean. Cool for 10 minutes in the pan, remove, and cool completely on a wire rack.
8. Serve cold with a little butter on the slices. This bread freezes well.

WHOLE WHEAT NUT QUICK BREAD

2 cups whole wheat flour
¼ cup bran flakes cereal
¼ cup wheat germ
2 teaspoons ground allspice
¼ teaspoon ground cloves
2 teaspoons baking powder
1 teaspoon baking soda
⅓ cup honey
½ cup plain or vanilla yogurt
½ cup apple sauce
½ cup apple juice or cider
⅓ cup vegetable oil
2 large eggs
1 cup chopped walnuts

This bread is packed with such nutritional goodness, eating a slice makes you feel as though you're doing your body a real favor. Eat it for breakfast, a snack, or at lunch. For a dinner bread, substitute the allspice with a mix of herbs such as basil, thyme, or oregano.

1. Preheat the oven to 350°F. Grease and flour a 9-inch by 5-inch loaf pan.
2. In a large bowl, combine the whole wheat flour, bran flakes, wheat germ, allspice, cloves, baking powder, and baking soda. Make a well in the center.
3. In a small bowl, mix together the honey, yogurt, apple sauce, apple juice, vegetable oil, and eggs. Beat well and pour into the center of the dry ingredients. Stir to combine without overmixing.
4. Fold in the chopped nuts and spoon the batter into the loaf pan.
5. Bake in the oven for 50–55 minutes, or until a skewer inserted in the center comes out clean. Cool in the pan on a wire rack for 10 minutes. Remove from the pan and cool completely on a wire rack.

BARBARA MULLIN'S APPLE COFFEE CAN BREAD

PREPARATION TIME: 25 MINUTES   BAKING TIME: 1¼ HOURS   YIELD: 3 CAKES, ABOUT 10 SLICES EACH

4 medium-size apples (Cortland, Northern Spy, Winesap)
2 cups sugar
1 cup coarsely chopped pecans
3 cups presifted all-purpose flour
2 teaspoons baking soda
½ teaspoon ground allspice
½ teaspoon ground nutmeg
1 teaspoon ground cinnamon
1 cup sweet butter or margarine
1 tablespoon vanilla extract
2 large eggs

1. Preheat the oven to 325°F. Grease and flour three 1-pound coffee cans. Tie a double band of aluminum foil around the cans to extend 2 inches above the edges of the cans. Grease the foil.
2. Peel, core, and finely dice the apples. Place in a large bowl and mix with the sugar and pecans.
3. Sift in the flour, baking soda, and spices. Mix well.
4. Melt the butter in a small saucepan and stir in the vanilla.
5. Lightly beat the eggs. Stir the eggs and butter into the apple mixture.
6. Spoon the batter into the cans and bake for 1¼ hours or until a skewer inserted in the center comes out clean. Cool in the cans for 10 minutes; remove to a wire rack to finish cooling.

BRAN APPLE SAUCE MUFFINS

PREPARATION TIME: 15 MINUTES   BAKING TIME: 20–25 MINUTES   YIELD: 12–18 MUFFINS

½ cup whole wheat flour
1 cup presifted all-purpose flour
1 cup bran flakes cereal
2 teaspoons baking powder
1 teaspoon baking soda
1 teaspoon ground cinnamon
½ teaspoon ground nutmeg
¼ teaspoon ground cloves
⅓ cup vegetable oil
1 cup apple sauce
2 large eggs
½ cup honey

1. Preheat the oven to 400°F. Grease 12 large or 18 shallow muffin cups.
2. In a large bowl, stir together the flours, bran flakes, baking powder, baking soda, and spices.
3. Make a well in the middle of the dry ingredients and pour in the oil and apple sauce.
4. In a small bowl, beat together the eggs and honey and add to the large bowl.
5. Stir together until the dry ingredients are moist (a lumpy mixture makes tender muffins). Fill each muffin cup approximately two-thirds full.
6. Bake for 20–25 minutes or until a skewer inserted in the center comes out clean. Remove from the muffin tray immediately and cool on a wire rack or serve hot.

CORNMEAL APPLE CHEESE MUFFINS

PREPARATION TIME: 20 MINUTES   BAKING TIME: 25 MINUTES   YIELD: 12–18 MUFFINS

¾ cup yellow cornmeal

1½ cups presifted all-purpose flour

2 teaspoons baking powder

1 teaspoon baking soda

½ teaspoon ground cinnamon

½ teaspoon ground nutmeg

¾ cup milk

¼ cup apple juice or cider

⅓ cup vegetable oil

2 large eggs

⅓ cup honey

¾ cup grated cheddar cheese

1 medium-size apple (Granny Smith)

1. Preheat the oven to 400°F. Grease 12 large or 18 shallow muffin cups.
2. In a large bowl, stir together the cornmeal, flour, baking powder, baking soda, cinnamon, and nutmeg.
3. In a small bowl, mix together the milk and apple juice.
4. Beat in the oil, eggs, and honey.
5. Make a well in the center of the dry ingredients and pour in the liquids and the grated cheese. Stir to barely combine.
6. Peel, core, and finely dice the apple. Stir into the other ingredients until the batter is lumpy, not smooth.
7. Fill each muffin cup approximately two-thirds full. Bake for 25 minutes or until a skewer, inserted in the center of a muffin, comes out clean. Remove from the muffin tray immediately and cool on a wire rack or serve hot.

HONEY CREAM CHEESE SPREAD

PREPARATION TIME: 5 MINUTES   YIELD: 1 CUP

8 ounces cream cheese, softened

2–4 tablespoons honey

1 teaspoon grated orange or lemon rind

1. Combine all of the ingredients. Beat well.
2. Spread on individual slices of quick breads.

APRICOT CREAM CHEESE SPREAD

PREPARATION TIME: 5 MINUTES   YIELD: 1¼ CUPS

8 ounces cream cheese, softened
¼ cup apricot preserves

1. Combine the cream cheese and preserves. Beat well.
2. Spread on individual slices of quick breads or use as a frosting.

APPLE DATE SPREAD

PREPARATION TIME: 10 MINUTES   YIELD: 1¾ CUPS

1 cup finely chopped pitted dates
½ cup apple juice or cider
8 ounces cream cheese, softened

1. In a small saucepan, cook the dates in the apple juice, simmering and stirring until the mixture thickens, about 5 minutes. Set aside to cool.
2. Meanwhile, beat the cream cheese until fluffy.
3. Beat the cooled date mixture into the cream cheese.
4. Chill and spread on individual slices of quick breads.

APPLE SPICE FROSTING

PREPARATION TIME: 5 MINUTES   YIELD: 3 CUPS

8 ounces cream cheese, softened
½ cup sweet butter, softened
1 cup confectioners' sugar
2 tablespoons apple juice
1 teaspoon (or to taste) ground
  cinnamon

1. Combine the cream cheese, butter, sugar, apple juice, and cinnamon. Beat until fluffy.
2. Spread on top of fruit breads or cakes.

APPLES
FOR DESSERT

If you were to set out and collect apple dessert recipes, you could quite easily go berserk. In my opinion, only an encyclopedia can do justice to all the apple desserts in creation.

After trying out more apple desserts than I care to remember, I still favor plain apple pie and, when I'm too busy or just too lazy to make pastry, any of the apple crisps. Of course, the cakes are superbly spicy, moist, and rich, and I always have found it difficult to resist crêpes . . .

APPLE MOLASSES COOKIES

PREPARATION TIME: 15 MINUTES, PLUS 1 HOUR CHILLING TIME   BAKING TIME: 10 MINUTES   YIELD: APPROXIMATELY 40 COOKIES

3 cups presifted all-purpose flour
1½ teaspoons ground ginger
½ teaspoon ground nutmeg
1 teaspoon baking soda
1 cup sweet butter or margarine, softened
1 cup dark brown sugar
2 large eggs
½ cup molasses
¼ cup apple juice or cider

1. In a medium-size bowl, mix together the flour, ginger, nutmeg, and baking soda.
2. In a large bowl, cream together the butter and sugar. Add the eggs and beat until combined.
3. Beat in the molasses and apple juice.
4. Stir in the flour mixture and beat until smooth.
5. Cover and refrigerate for approximately 1 hour.
6. Preheat the oven to 375°F. and grease 2 large cookie sheets.
7. Using a tablespoon, drop the dough 2 inches apart onto the baking trays. Bake for 10 minutes or until the cookies are lightly browned around the edges. Remove from the trays and cool on wire racks.

APPLE WHEAT GERM COOKIES

PREPARATION TIME: 25 MINUTES   BAKING TIME: 12–15 MINUTES   YIELD: 36 COOKIES

1 large apple (Cortland)
⅓ cup sweet butter or margarine, softened
⅓ cup honey
2 large eggs, separated
2 tablespoons wheat germ
½ cup presifted all-purpose flour
½ cup whole wheat flour
1 teaspoon ground cinnamon
½ teaspoon nutmeg

1. Preheat the oven to 350°F. Grease 2 large cookie sheets.
2. Core and grate the apple into a small bowl. Reserve.
3. Cream the butter and honey together in a medium-size bowl.
4. Beat in the egg yolks. Stir in the grated apple.
5. Mix the wheat germ, flours, and spices together. Stir into the apple mixture.
6. Beat the egg whites until stiff. Fold into the batter.
7. Drop by the teaspoonful onto the greased cookie sheets, about 2 inches apart.
8. Bake for 12–15 minutes or until lightly browned around the edges. Remove onto racks to cool.

APPLE FLAPJACK COOKIES

PREPARATION TIME: 25 MINUTES   BAKING TIME: 20 MINUTES   YIELD: 32 COOKIES

4 tablespoons sweet butter or margarine
¼ cup dark brown sugar
2 tablespoons honey
1 cup rolled oats
2 tablespoons sweet butter or margarine
3 medium-size apples (McIntosh, Golden Delicious, Macoun)
¼ cup sugar

1. Preheat the oven to 350°F. Grease and flour an 8-inch by 8-inch baking dish.
2. Melt the 4 tablespoons butter in a medium-size saucepan. Stir in the brown sugar, honey, and oats.
3. Turn into the prepared baking dish and spread over the bottom and up the sides. Bake in the oven for 10 minutes.
4. In the saucepan, melt the remaining 2 tablespoons butter.
5. Peel, core, and thinly slice the apples. Add to the butter in the saucepan, cover, and cook for 10 minutes, or until soft.
6. Stir in the granulated sugar, beat until the mixture is smooth, and cook over low heat for 5 minutes.
7. Spoon the apple mixture over the baked oat base and bake for another 20 minutes.
8. Cool in the pan on a wire rack. Slice into squares when completely cooled.

APPLE KUCHEN

PREPARATION TIME: 20 MINUTES   BAKING TIME: 35 MINUTES   YIELD: 12 SERVINGS

1¼ cups all-purpose flour
1½ teaspoons baking powder
½ cup sugar
¼ cup sweet butter or margarine
1 large egg
¼ cup apple juice or cider
1 tablespoon vanilla extract
2 large apples (Northern Spy, Idared, Cortland, Rome Beauty)
½ cup pecan halves
¼ cup sweet butter or margarine
¼ cup honey

1. Preheat the oven to 400°F. Grease a 9-inch by 13-inch baking dish.
2. In a medium-size bowl, combine the flour, baking powder, and sugar. Cut in ¼ cup butter until the mixture resembles crumbs.
3. Beat together the egg, apple juice, and vanilla extract. Stir into the crumb mixture.
4. Spread the batter into the prepared dish.
5. Peel, core, and cut the apples into ½-inch slices. Arrange on top of the batter.
6. Dot the apple slices with the pecan halves.
7. Melt the remaining ¼ cup butter and the honey in a small saucepan. Pour over the apples and pecans.
8. Bake for 35 minutes. Serve warm.

OATMEAL APPLE CUPCAKES

PREPARATION TIME: 15 MINUTES   BAKING TIME: 20 MINUTES   YIELD: 24 CUPCAKES

½ cup sweet butter or margarine, softened
½ cup light brown sugar
½ cup honey
2 large eggs
1 cup apple sauce
1 cup presifted all-purpose flour
½ cup whole wheat flour
1½ teaspoons baking powder
1 teaspoon baking soda
1 teaspoon ground allspice
1 cup rolled oats

1. Preheat the oven to 375°F. Line 24 muffin cups with paper liners.
2. In a medium-size bowl, cream together the butter and sugar.
3. Beat in the honey, eggs, and apple sauce.
4. Mix together the flours, baking powder, baking soda, allspice, and oats. Stir into the apple sauce mixture.
5. Fill the paper cups half full with the batter. Bake for 20 minutes or until a skewer inserted in the center of a cupcake comes out clean. Remove from the muffin pans and cool on wire racks. Frost with the Apple Glaze (page 86), if desired.

APPLE DATE CUPCAKES

PREPARATION TIME: 20 MINUTES   BAKING TIME: 20 MINUTES   YIELD: 36 CUPCAKES

½ cup sweet butter or margarine,
  softened
1 cup brown sugar
2 tablespoons apple juice or
  cider
2 large eggs
1 cup chopped pitted dates
2 small apples (McIntosh,
  Golden Delicious)
2 cups presifted all-purpose flour
1 teaspoon baking soda
1 teaspoon baking powder
½ teaspoon ground nutmeg
½ teaspoon ground ginger

1. Preheat the oven to 350°F. Line 36 muffin cups with paper liners.
2. In a medium-size bowl, cream the butter and sugar together.
3. Beat in the apple juice and eggs. Stir in the dates.
4. Peel, core, and grate the apples directly into the bowl. Stir to combine.
5. Mix together the flour, baking soda, baking powder, nutmeg, and ginger. Stir into the batter.
6. Fill the paper cups half full with the batter. Bake for 20 minutes or until a skewer inserted in the center comes out clean. Remove from the muffin trays and cool on wire racks. Frost with the Apple Glaze, if desired.

APPLE GLAZE

PREPARATION TIME: 10 MINUTES   YIELD: GLAZE FOR 2 CAKES, 48 CUPCAKES

4 teaspoons cornstarch
1 cup apple juice or cider
1 cup frozen apple juice
  concentrate
1 teaspoon ground cinnamon
½ cup confectioners' sugar
  (optional)

If a glaze is desired for the Apple Date or the Oatmeal Apple Cupcakes, the following recipe will prove to be a winner.

1. Mix the cornstarch with a drop of the apple juice to make a smooth paste. Gradually stir into the rest of the juice in a small saucepan.
2. Cook over low heat, stirring all the time, until thick and smooth.
3. Stir in the apple concentrate and cinnamon. Remove from the heat. For a sweeter glaze, beat in the confectioners' sugar.
4. Cool a little and spoon over a slightly warm cake.

CHOCOLATE APPLE SAUCE CAKE

PREPARATION TIME: 25 MINUTES   BAKING TIME: 70 MINUTES   YIELD: 20 SERVINGS

¼ cup graham cracker crumbs
8 ounces semi-sweet chocolate
1 cup sweet butter, softened
1½ cups dark brown sugar
4 large eggs
1½ cups presifted all-purpose
flour
2 teaspoons baking powder
1 teaspoon baking soda
½ teaspoon ground cinnamon
2 tablespoons cocoa
1½ cups apple sauce

1. Grease a 9-inch springform pan and dust with graham cracker crumbs.
2. Place the chocolate in a small ovenproof bowl and place in the oven. Turn the oven thermostat to 350°F. and remove the chocolate after 10 minutes to finish melting in the hot bowl.
3. Cream the butter and sugar until fluffy. Add the eggs, one at a time, and beat until combined.
4. Beat in the melted chocolate.
5. Sift together the flour, baking powder, baking soda, cinnamon, and cocoa.
6. Stir approximately ½ cup of the flour mixture and ½ cup of the apple sauce into the butter mixture. Continue to combine the ingredients until all has been mixed into the batter.
7. Spoon the batter into the prepared pan and bake for 70 minutes, or until a skewer inserted in the center comes out clean.
8. Allow to cool for 10 minutes in the pan on a wire rack. The cake will shrink. Use a knife to loosen the cake before releasing the spring and lifting the sides off the bottom of the pan. Serve cooled.

APPLE COFFEE CAKE

PREPARATION TIME: 30 MINUTES   BAKING TIME: 1⅓ HOURS   YIELD: 15–20 SERVINGS

3 medium-size apples (Golden
  Delicious)
½ lemon
1 teaspoon ground cinnamon
1 cup sweet butter, softened
2 cups sugar
4 large eggs
1 cup sour cream
1 tablespoon vanilla extract
2½ cups presifted all-purpose
  flour
1 teaspoon baking powder
1 teaspoon baking soda
1 tablespoon ground cinnamon
½ cup brown sugar
1 cup chopped pecans

1. Preheat the oven to 350°F. Grease and flour a 10-inch tube pan.
2. Peel, core, and chop the apples into small pieces. Place in a large bowl and toss with the juice from the lemon and 1 teaspoon cinnamon.
3. In a large mixing bowl, cream the butter and sugar until fluffy. Beat in the eggs, sour cream, and vanilla extract.
4. Sift the flour, baking powder, and baking soda together. Fold into the sour cream mixture.
5. Stir in the chopped apples. Pour half of this batter into the prepared tube pan.
6. In a small bowl, mix the remaining 1 tablespoon cinnamon, the brown sugar, and chopped pecans together. Sprinkle over the batter in the baking pan. Cover with the rest of the batter and smooth the top.
7. Bake for 1⅓ hours, or until a skewer inserted in the middle comes out clean.
8. Remove from the oven and allow to cool for 10 minutes in the pan. Turn onto a wire rack and allow to cool completely before cutting into the cake.

APPLE LEMON CAKE

PREPARATION TIME: 40 MINUTES   BAKING TIME: 1⅓ HOURS   YIELD: 15–20 SERVINGS

3 medium-size apples (Winesap, Mutsu, Macoun)
1 medium-size lemon
1 cup sweet butter or margarine, melted
½ cup vegetable oil
3 large eggs
2 cups sugar
3 cups presifted all-purpose flour
1 teaspoon baking soda
1 teaspoon baking powder
1 cup chopped pecans
1 cup confectioners' sugar
2 tablespoons sweet butter or margarine, softened
3 tablespoons lemon juice
1 teaspoon grated lemon rind
1 tablespoon honey

1. Preheat the oven to 350°F. Grease and flour a 10-inch tube pan.
2. Peel, core, and chop the apples. Place in a bowl.
3. Grate the rind off the lemon, or peel thinly with a knife and process in a food processor. Reserve.
4. Squeeze the juice of the lemon over the chopped apple and toss to coat each piece.
5. Pour the melted butter or margarine into a large mixing bowl.
6. Add the oil and beat in the eggs, one at a time.
7. Beat in the sugar and 3 teaspoons of grated lemon rind.
8. Sift together the flour, baking soda, and baking powder. Stir into the batter.
9. Fold in the chopped pecans and apples.
10. Pour the batter into the prepared baking pan and bake for 1⅓ hours, or until a skewer inserted in the middle comes out clean.
11. Remove from the oven and allow to cool 10 minutes in the pan. Turn onto a wire rack.
12. Prepare a glaze by sifting the confectioners' sugar into a small bowl and beating in the 2 tablespoons of softened sweet butter, 3 tablespoons of lemon juice, 1 teaspoon of grated lemon rind, and 1 tablespoon of honey. Spread over the warm cake after pricking the top with a fork.

APPLE SAUCE GINGERBREAD

PREPARATION TIME: 20 MINUTES   BAKING TIME: 35 MINUTES   YIELD: 18 SERVINGS

1 cup sweet butter or margarine
1 cup brown sugar
½ cup molasses
2 large eggs
1 cup apple sauce
2 cups all-purpose flour
2 teaspoons baking soda
2 teaspoons ground ginger
1 teaspoon ground cinnamon

1. Preheat the oven to 350°F. Grease and flour a 9-inch by 13-inch baking dish.
2. Melt the butter over low heat. Pour into a medium-size bowl.
3. Beat in the sugar and molasses. Add the eggs one at a time and beat.
4. Beat in the apple sauce.
5. Sift the flour, baking soda, ginger, and cinnamon into the apple sauce mixture and stir well to combine thoroughly.
6. Spoon into the baking dish and bake for 35 minutes, or until a skewer inserted in the middle comes out clean.
7. Remove from the oven and allow to cool for 5 minutes. Turn onto a wire rack and allow to cool completely.
8. Serve with whipped cream or vanilla ice cream.

MAPLE APPLE CRISP

PREPARATION TIME: 20 MINUTES   BAKING TIME: 40 MINUTES   YIELD: 6–8 SERVIINGS

1 cup granola
½ cup rolled oats
½ cup chopped walnuts or pecans
½ cup dark brown sugar
1 teaspoon ground cinnamon
½ cup sweet butter or margarine
4 large apples (Winesap, Idared, Northern Spy)
1 tablespoon lemon juice
⅓ cup maple syrup

1. Preheat the oven to 400°F. and grease a deep 2-quart baking dish.
2. In a medium-size bowl, combine the granola, oats, walnuts, brown sugar, and cinnamon. Rub in the butter.
3. Peel, core, and cut the apples into ¼-inch slices. Place in the baking dish and sprinkle with the lemon juice and maple syrup.
4. Cover completely with the granola mixture and bake for 40 minutes or until the apples are tender when pierced with a thin skewer. Serve warm with heavy cream.

APPLE BLACKBERRY CRISP

PREPARATION TIME: 20 MINUTES   BAKING TIME: 30 MINUTES   YIELD: 8 SERVINGS

4 large apples (Rome Beauty,
   Winesap, Idared)
1½–2 cups blackberries
½ cup sugar
2 tablespoons all-purpose flour
1 cup all-purpose flour
½ cup brown sugar
1 teaspoon cinnamon
½ cup sweet butter or margarine

There are pounds of blackberries for the picking on the hills behind my mother's house in Argyll, Scotland. Although most are used for jam and jelly making, some find their way into dessert dishes. This is one of them.

1. Preheat the oven to 400°F. Grease a deep 2-quart casserole.
2. Peel, core, and slice the apples into ¼-inch-thick pieces. Cook over low heat for 10 minutes. Place in the baking dish, add the blackberries.
3. Combine ½ cup sugar and 2 tablespoons flour. Mix into the apple slices and blackberries.
4. In a medium-size bowl, mix together the remaining 1 cup flour, brown sugar, and cinnamon. Cut in the butter until the mixture resembles coarse crumbs.
5. Sprinkle over the apple filling and bake for 30 minutes or until the crumbs are golden brown. Serve warm with English Custard Sauce (page 105) or heavy cream.

TOM CARROLAN'S APPLE CRISP

PREPARATION TIME: 25 MINUTES   BAKING TIME: 60 MINUTES   YIELD: 8–10 SERVINGS

9–10 medium-size apples
  (Northern Spy)
2 tablespoons honey
¼ cup apple juice or cider
1 cup light brown sugar
¾ cup all-purpose flour
½ teaspoon ground cinnamon
½ teaspoon ground nutmeg
½ cup sweet butter

Tom belonged to my Bedford Audubon birding group. After testing some of my recipes on a number of our outings, he finally gave me his recipe for "the best apple crisp." Tom serves his crisp warm with heavy cream. It is sinfully delicious.

1. Preheat the oven to 350°F. Grease a 2-quart casserole.
2. Peel, core, and thinly slice the apples. Place in the dish, drizzle with honey, and add the apple juice.
3. Mix the sugar, flour, and spices in a small bowl. Cut in the butter until the mixture resembles coarse crumbs. Sprinkle over the apples.
4. Cover the casserole with aluminum foil and bake for 30 minutes. Remove the foil and continue baking for another 30 minutes.

APPLE AND DATE SQUARES

PREPARATION TIME: 20 MINUTES   BAKING TIME: 30 MINUTES   YIELD: 16 SQUARES

½ cup sweet butter or margarine,
  softened
1 cup brown sugar
2 large eggs
1 cup presifted all-purpose flour
½ teaspoon baking powder
½ teaspoon baking soda
1 teaspoon ground cinnamon
¼ teaspoon ground cloves
¼ teaspoon ground nutmeg
1 large apple (Twenty Ounce,
  Northern Spy, Winesap)
1 cup dates
½ cup chopped walnuts

1. Preheat the oven to 350°F. Grease and flour an 8-inch by 8-inch baking dish.
2. In a medium-size bowl, cream together the softened butter and sugar until fluffy.
3. Beat in the eggs, one at a time.
4. Sift in the flour, baking powder, baking soda, and the spices. Stir to combine.
5. Peel, core, and chop the apple. Chop the dates and stir both fruits into the batter.
6. Stir in the walnuts. Pour into the prepared baking dish.
7. Bake in the oven for 30 minutes or until a skewer inserted in the center comes out clean. Cool in the pan on a wire rack. When cooled, slice into squares.

APPLE SAUCE BROWNIES

PREPARATION TIME: 20 MINUTES   BAKING TIME: 25–30 MINUTES   YIELD: 16 SERVINGS

½ cup sweet butter or margarine
1½ cups brown sugar
2 large eggs
1 tablespoon vanilla extract
1 cup apple sauce
1¼ cups presifted all-purpose flour
¼ cup cocoa
1 teaspoon baking powder
½ teaspoon baking soda
½ cup chopped pecans

1. Preheat the oven to 350°F. Grease and flour an 8-inch by 8-inch baking dish.
2. Melt the butter in a 2½-quart saucepan. Remove from the heat and beat in the sugar, eggs, vanilla, and apple sauce.
3. Sift in the flour, cocoa, baking powder, and baking soda. Stir to combine.
4. Stir in the chopped pecans.
5. Pour the batter into the prepared baking dish and bake for 25–30 minutes, or until a skewer inserted in the center comes out clean. Cool in the pan on a wire rack. Slice into squares.

NANCY BLACK'S SCHOOL BROWNIES

PREPARATION TIME: 20 MINUTES   BAKING TIME: 30 MINUTES   YIELD: 16 SERVINGS

½ cup margarine at room temperature
1 cup sugar
1 large egg
1 cup presifted all-purpose flour
½ teaspoon baking soda
1½ teaspoons baking powder
½ teaspoon ground cinnamon
¼ teaspoon ground nutmeg
1 large apple (Rome Beauty)
3/4 cup chopped walnuts
1 teaspoon vanilla extract

My daughter Wendy brought home one of her teacher's brownies in her lunch box. It was so delicious, I asked for the recipe. Here it is.

1. Preheat the oven to 350°F. Grease and flour an 8-inch by 8-inch baking dish.
2. Cream together the margarine and sugar in a medium-size bowl.
3. Beat in the egg.
4. In another bowl, mix together the flour, baking soda, baking powder, and spices. Stir into the batter.
5. Peel, core, and dice the apple. Add to the batter with the chopped walnuts and vanilla extract. Stir to combine.
6. Pour into the baking dish and bake for 30 minutes or until a skewer inserted in the middle comes out clean. Cool in the pan on a wire rack. Slice into squares.

APPLE-CINNAMON SQUARES

PREPARATION TIME: 25 MINUTES   BAKING TIME: 30 MINUTES   YIELD: 16 SQUARES

½ cup sweet butter or margarine
¾ cup brown sugar
2 large eggs
1 tablespoon vanilla extract
⅓ cup whole wheat flour
⅔ cup presifted all-purpose flour
1 teaspoon baking powder
½ teaspoon baking soda
1 teaspoons ground cinnamon
1 large apple (Rome Beauty)
½ cup raisins
2 tablespoons ground cinnamon
½ cup sugar
2 tablespoons sweet butter or
  margarine

1. Preheat the oven to 350°F. Grease and flour an 8-inch by 8-inch baking dish.
2. Melt ½ cup butter in a 2½-quart saucepan. Remove from the heat and stir in the brown sugar.
3. Beat in the eggs, one at a time. Add the vanilla extract.
4. Stir in the whole wheat flour. Sift in the all-purpose flour, baking powder, baking soda, and 1½ teaspoons cinnamon. Stir together.
5. Peel, core, and dice the apple. Add to the batter with the raisins and stir to combine. Pour into the baking dish.
6. Mix together the remaining 2 tablespoons cinnamon and the ½ cup sugar. Sprinkle over the top of the batter.
7. Melt the remaining 2 tablespoons butter and drizzle over sugar and cinnamon.
8. Bake in the oven for 30 minutes or until a skewer inserted in the center comes out clean. Remove and cool in the pan on a wire rack. When cool, slice into squares.

APPLE-RHUBARB SLUMP

PREPARATION TIME: 20 MINUTES   BAKING TIME: 25–30 MINUTES   YIELD: 8 SERVINGS

4 medium-size apples (McIntosh, Golden Delicious)
2 cups rhubarb stems, cut in 1-inch pieces
¾ cup sugar
½ teaspoon ground cinnamon
½ teaspoon ground ginger
¼ teaspoon ground cloves
1 cup all-purpose flour
1½ teaspoons baking powder
2 tablespoons sugar
3 tablespoons sweet butter or margarine
½ cup milk
1 tablespoon vanilla extract

Slump is a New England name for a fruit dessert topped with a sweet dumpling mixture. On Cape Cod, traditionalists call slumps grunts. In other parts of the country, they fall under the heading of cobblers. No matter what they're called, they all taste good.

1. Preheat the oven to 400°F. Grease a 2-quart baking dish.
2. Peel, core, and slice the apples into ½-inch pieces. Place in a saucepan and add the rhubarb, ¾ cup sugar, and the spices. Cover the pan and cook over low heat for about 10 minutes, stirring once or twice, until the apple slices are tender but not falling apart.
3. In a medium-size bowl, sift the flour and baking powder. Stir in the remaining 2 tablespoons sugar. Cut in the butter until the mixture resembles crumbs.
4. Stir the milk and vanilla extract into the crumb mixture until just blended. Do not overmix.
5. Pour the hot apple-rhubarb mixture into the greased dish and spoon the dough in dollops over the top.
6. Bake for 25–30 minutes, until golden. Serve warm with English Custard Sauce (page 105) or heavy cream.

95

APPLE APRICOT COBBLER

PREPARATION TIME: 30 MINUTES   BAKING TIME: 40 MINUTES   YIELD: 8 SERVINGS

1 cup dried apricots
½ cup orange juice
5 large apples (Golden Delicious)
½ cup dark brown sugar
½ teaspoon ground allspice
¼ teaspoon ground ginger
¼ teaspoon ground cloves
¾ cup sweet butter or margarine,
    softened
¾ cup sugar
2 large eggs
1 tablespoon vanilla extract
1½ cups presifted all-purpose
    flour
2 teaspoons baking powder
1 tablespoon brown sugar

1. Halve the dried apricots, place in a medium-size saucepan, and cover with the orange juice.
2. Preheat the oven to 375°F. Grease a 2-quart or 2½-quart baking dish
3. Peel, core, and cut the apples in ¼-inch slices. Add to the apricots along with the brown sugar and spices. Mix together and simmer for 10 minutes.
4. In a medium-size bowl, beat the softened butter and sugar until fluffy. Beat in the eggs, one at a time. Stir in the vanilla extract.
5. Stir the flour and baking powder into the bowl and beat until blended.
6. Turn the apple mixture into the baking dish and cover with the batter. Sprinkle the top with 1 tablespoon of brown sugar.
7. Bake for 40 minutes, or until the crust is golden brown.

BARBARA MULLIN'S APPLE COBBLER

PREPARATION TIME: 15 MINUTES   BAKING TIME: 45 MINUTES   YIELD: 8 SERVINGS

6 large apples (Jonathan)
1 cup flour
1 teaspoon ground cinnamon
1 teaspoon baking powder
½ cup sugar
½ cup brown sugar
1 large egg
⅓ cup sweet butter or margarine

Working as she does everyday at the Haight Orchard in Croton Falls, New York, Barbara does not have much time for fancy cooking. Her recipe for apple cobbler is simple and superb.

1. Preheat the oven to 350°F. Grease a 2-quart baking dish.
2. Peel, core, and slice the apples into ¼-inch pieces.
3. In a medium-size bowl, mix the flour, cinnamon, baking powder, and the sugars. Beat the egg lightly and stir into the sugar mixture. Spoon on top of the sliced apples.
4. Melt the butter in a small pan and drizzle over the batter.
5. Bake for 45 minutes.

APPLE BROWN BETTY

PREPARATION TIME: 25 MINUTES   BAKING TIME: 50 MINUTES   YIELD: 8 SERVINGS

¾ cup brown sugar
1 teaspoon ground cinnamon
½ teaspoon ground nutmeg
¼ teaspoon ground cloves
6 slices bread
½ cup sweet butter or margarine
3 tablespoons lemon juice
4 large apples (Rome Beauty, Winesap, Cortland)
¼ cup apple juice or cider

1. Preheat the oven to 350°F. Grease a 2-quart baking dish.
2. In a large bowl, mix together the sugar, cinnamon, nutmeg, and cloves. Crumble in the slices of bread.
3. Melt the butter, add the lemon juice, and stir into the crumbled bread mixture.
4. Peel, core, and thinly slice the apples.
5. Cover the bottom of the baking dish with a layer of the crumbs (about one-third of the mixture), add half the apples, a layer of crumbs, the rest of the apples, and finally the remaining crumbs.
6. Pour the apple juice over the top, cover with foil, and bake for 30 minutes. Remove the cover and bake 20 minutes longer. Serve warm.

ENGLISH APPLE CRUMBLE

PREPARATION TIME: 20 MINUTES   BAKING TIME: 30 MINUTES   YIELD: 8 SERVINGS

6 medium-size tart apples
(Granny Smith, Rhode Island
Greening, Twenty Ounce)
⅓ cup sugar
1 teaspoon ground cinnamon
Juice of ½ lemon
¾ cup all-purpose flour
¼ cup sugar
4 tablespoons sweet butter or
margarine

This is my mother's recipe. A crumble is like a crisp, but not as rich.

1. Preheat the oven to 400°F. Grease a 2-quart baking dish.
2. Peel, core, and slice the apples into ½-inch pieces. Place in a saucepan with ⅓ cup sugar, cinnamon, and lemon juice. Cook over low heat, stirring once or twice, for 10 minutes, or until the apple slices are tender but not falling apart. Spoon into the baking dish.
3. Combine the flour and the remaining ¼ cup sugar in a small bowl. Cut in the butter until the mixture is crumbly. Sprinkle on top of the apples. (I like to sprinkle the crumbs with 2 teaspoons sugar.)
4. Bake for 30 minutes or until the topping is golden brown.

APPLE RAISIN CRUNCH

PREPARATION TIME: 20 MINUTES   BAKING TIME: 30 MINUTES   YIELD: 8 SERVINGS

4 medium-size apples (Granny
Smith, Newtown Pippin,
Northern Spy)
1 cup golden raisins
2 tablespoons brown sugar
1 teaspoon grated orange rind
¼ cup orange juice
1 teaspoon ground allspice
1 cup all-purpose flour
1 cup brown sugar
¾ cup rolled oats
½ teaspoon ground cinnamon
½ cup sweet butter or margarine

For a really decadent crunch, crisp, or cobbler, drizzle a few tablespoons of melted butter over the top before popping it in the oven.

1. Preheat the oven to 400°F. Grease a 2-quart baking dish.
2. Peel, core, and slice the apples into ¼-inch-thick pieces.
3. Combine with the raisins, 2 tablespoons brown sugar, orange rind, orange juice, and allspice in the baking dish.
4. In a medium-size bowl, mix together the flour, the remaining 1 cup brown sugar, oats, and cinnamon. Cut in the butter until the mixture is crumbly. Sprinkle on top of the apples and raisins.
5. Bake in the oven for 30 minutes or until the topping is golden.

ORANGE BAKED APPLES

PREPARATION TIME: 20 MINUTES   BAKING TIME: 60 MINUTES   YIELD: 4 SERVINGS

4 medium-size apples (Baldwin, Granny Smith, Rhode Island Greening)

¼ cup sweet butter or margarine, softened

2 tablespoons sugar

1 tablespoon vanilla extract

½ cup stale cake crumbs

1 small juice orange

½ cup apple juice or cider

2 tablespoons brown sugar

1. Preheat the oven to 350°F. Grease a baking dish.
2. Core the apples three-quarters of the way down. Remove a ½-inch strip of peel off the top (or make a horizontal slit all the way around about one-third of the way down).
3. Beat together the softened butter, sugar, and the vanilla extract. Stir in the cake crumbs.
4. Stuff into the center of each apple and fit snugly into the baking dish.
5. Grate the orange rind into a small bowl, cut the orange in half, and squeeze the juice on top. Add the apple juice. Stir together and pour over the apples.
6. Cover the dish with aluminum foil and bake for 45 minutes. Remove the foil, sprinkle with the brown sugar, and continue baking for 15 minutes. Serve warm.

STEAMED APPLES

PREPARATION TIME: 15 MINUTES   COOKING TIME: 15 MINUTES   YIELD: 4 SERVINGS

4 medium-size apples (Golden Delicious, Granny Smith, Jonathan)

¼ cup marmalade

2 tablespoons chopped nuts

½ teaspoon ground ginger

½ teaspoon ground nutmeg

1. Pour approximately 2 cups water into the base of a steamer.
2. Core the apples three-quarters of the way down. Remove a ½-inch strip of peel off the top part or make a horizontal slit all the way around about one-third of the way down. Place on a dish that fits in the steamer.
3. Mix together the marmalade, nuts, and spices. Put a tablespoon or so in the core of each apple.
4. Place the dish of apples in the top of the steamer, cover, and bring the water to a boil. Steam for 15 minutes, or until the apples are tender. Serve warm.

MERINGUE-BAKED APPLES

PREPARATION TIME: 15 MINUTES   BAKING TIME: 40 MINUTES   YIELD: 8 SERVINGS

4 medium-size apples (Jonathan,
  Idared, Granny Smith)
¼ cup apple juice or cider
¼ cup honey
2 tablespoons sweet butter or
  margarine
½ teaspoon ground cinnamon
½ teaspoon ground nutmeg
3 egg whites, at room
  temperature
¼ teaspoon cream of tartar
¼ cup sugar

1. Preheat the oven to 350°F. Grease a 9-inch by 13-inch baking dish.
2. Core the apples. Cut into halves and arrange, cut side up, in the pan.
3. Combine the apple juice, honey, butter, and spices in a small saucepan. Heat and stir until the butter has melted. Pour over the apples.
4. Cover with aluminum foil and place in the oven. Bake for 15 minutes. Remove the foil and continue baking for 15 more minutes, or until tender.
5. In a wide bowl, beat the egg whites with the cream of tartar until foamy. Add the sugar, a little at a time, and continue beating until peaks form.
6. Spoon the meringue over each warm apple half and bake for 10 minutes, or until the meringue is tinged golden brown. Serve warm.

BAKED APPLE SLICES

PREPARATION TIME: 15 MINUTES   BAKING TIME: 35 MINUTES   YIELD: 6–8 SERVINGS

6 large apples (Mutsu, Jonagold,
  Idared, Rome Beauty)
½ cup brown sugar or maple
  sugar
¼ cup presifted all-purpose flour
1 teaspoon ground cinnamon
¼ teaspoon ground cloves
¼ teaspoon ground ginger
¼ cup sweet butter or margarine
¼ cup apple juice or cider

1. Preheat the oven to 350°F. Grease a large baking dish.
2. Core the apples. Cut each into 6 wedges and arrange in a single layer in the baking pan.
3. Mix the sugar, flour, and spices together. Sprinkle over the apples.
4. Melt the butter and mix with the apple juice. Pour over the top and toss to combine. Cover with aluminum foil.
5. Bake for 20 minutes. Uncover and bake for another 15 minutes. Serve warm.

APPLE AND VANILLA SOUFFLÉ

PREPARATION TIME: 50 MINUTES   BAKING TIME: 15 MINUTES   YIELD: 8 SERVINGS

4 medium-size apples (Idared, Empire, Golden Delicious)

4 tablespoons sweet butter

⅓ cup sugar

1 teaspoon ground cinnamon

⅔ cup milk

3 tablespoons sweet butter

3 tablespoons presifted all-purpose flour

¼ cup sugar

5 eggs, at room temperature

1 tablespoon vanilla extract

¼ teaspoon cream of tartar

1 tablespoon confectioners' sugar (optional)

1. Preheat the oven to 400°F. Grease a shallow 1½-quart baking dish.

2. Peel, core, and slice the apples into ½-inch pieces. In a skillet, melt 4 tablespoons butter and sauté the apples for 5 minutes over medium heat.

3. Mix ⅓ cup sugar and the cinnamon together. Sprinkle over the apples and stir to combine.

4. Continue to sauté the apples until they begin to caramelize, about 10 minutes. The mixture will be thick and syrupy and the apples tender. Remove from the heat and spoon into the baking dish.

5. Place the milk and the remaining 3 tablespoons butter in a small saucepan and bring almost to a boil. Remove from the heat.

6. Measure the flour and the remaining ¼ cup sugar into a bowl or blender.

7. Separate the eggs, pouring the whites into a large bowl and the yolks into a small bowl with the vanilla.

8. Beat the egg yolks and vanilla. Pour into the flour and sugar and blend. Pour in the hot milk and butter and blend or beat for 30 seconds. Return the mixture to the pan and cook over low heat for 2 minutes, or until the mixture thickens, stirring all the time. Do not overcook, or the eggs will scramble.

9. Using a wire whip or an electric beater, beat the whites with the cream of tartar until they stand up in smooth, shiny peaks. Stir one-third into the egg yolk mixture, then carefully and quickly fold in the rest.

10. Spoon the soufflé over the apple base and place in the preheated oven. Bake for 15 minutes (it will be puffed and golden). Remove and serve immediately. Sprinkle with the confectioners' sugar, if desired.

APPLE-CINNAMON SOUFFLÉ

PREPARATION TIME: 20 MINUTES   BAKING TIME: 35–40 MINUTES   YIELD: 4 SERVINGS

¾ cup milk

3 tablespoons sweet butter

3 tablespoons presifted all-
purpose flour

¼ cup sugar

2 teaspoons ground cinnamon

5 large eggs, at room
temperature

¼ teaspoon cream of tartar

1 cup apple sauce

1. Preheat the oven to 375°F. Grease a 1-quart soufflé mold. Take a piece of aluminum foil long enough to go around the outside of the mold and tall enough to extend 3 inches above the mold. Grease the inside of the foil then tie or pin in place.

2. Place the milk and butter in a small saucepan and bring almost to a boil.

3. Measure the flour, sugar, and cinnamon into a bowl or blender.

4. Separate the eggs. Pour the whites into a large metal, glass, or porcelain bowl and the yolks into the dry ingredients.

5. Beat or blend the yolks and flour. Pour in the hot milk and butter. Blend or beat for 30 seconds. Return to the pan and cook over low heat for 2 minutes, or until the mixture thickens, stirring continuously.

6. Mix in the apple sauce.

7. Using a wire whip or an electric beater, beat the whites with the cream of tartar until they stand up in smooth, shiny peaks. Stir a third into the soufflé base, then carefully and quickly fold in the rest until it is evenly distributed, but not deflated.

8. Pour into the prepared soufflé mold and bake for 35–40 minutes. Remove the collar gently and serve immediately.

APPLE SNOW

PREPARATION TIME: 10 MINUTES   YIELD: 6–8 SERVINGS

2 large egg whites
2 tablespoons confectioners' sugar
½ cup heavy cream
2 cups apple sauce
½ cup finely chopped blanched almonds or 2 tablespoons chopped crystalized ginger

1. Using electric beaters, whip the egg whites in a medium-size bowl until foamy. Add the confectioners' sugar and continue beating until the whites are stiff.
2. Pour the cream into a medium-size bowl and beat until stiff. Gently stir in the apple sauce.
3. Fold the stiff egg whites, one third at a time, into the sauce mixture.
4. Gently stir in the almonds or ginger. Chill at least 1 hour.

APPLE SPICE PUDDING

PREPARATION TIME: 25 MINUTES   BAKING TIME: 60 MINUTES   YIELD: 6–8 SERVINGS

8 slices oatmeal or whole wheat bread
1 cup milk
¼ cup apple juice or cider
2 tablespoons brown sugar
2 medium-size apples (Rome Beauty)
1 cup whole pitted dates or dried figs
½ cup sugar
½ teaspoon ground cloves
½ teaspoon ground ginger
¼ cup sweet butter or margarine
3 tablespoons marmalade
1 large egg

1. Preheat the oven to 350°F. Grease an 8-inch by 8-inch baking dish.
2. Place the bread in a bowl and cover with the milk and apple juice.
3. Sprinkle the brown sugar over the bottom of the greased dish.
4. Peel and core the apples. Slice one into ¼-inch rings and arrange in a single layer on top of the brown sugar. Dice the second apple and stir into the softened bread.
5. Chop the dates or figs and add to the apples and bread with the sugar, cloves, and ginger.
6. Melt the butter in a small saucepan and stir in the marmalade. Beat in the egg and combine with the bread mixture.
7. Spoon over the apple slices, level, and bake for 1 hour or until golden brown, and a knife inserted in the center comes out clean. Serve warm with English Custard Sauce (page 105).

APPLE SPONGE PUDDING

PREPARATION TIME: 25 MINUTES   BAKING TIME: 50–60 MINUTES   YIELD: 6–8 SERVINGS

3 medium-size apples (Golden Delicious, Idared, Empire)
⅓ cup honey or maple syrup
1 cup sweet butter or margarine, softened
1 cup sugar
4 large eggs
3 tablespoons lemon juice
2 cups presifted all-purpose flour
2 teaspoons baking powder
½ teaspoon baking soda
2 tablespoons brown sugar
1 teaspoon grated lemon rind
½ teaspoon ground cinnamon

1. Preheat the oven to 350°F. Grease a 1½-quart or 2-quart deep baking dish.
2. Peel, core, and slice the apples into ¼-inch pieces and place in the bottom of the dish.
3. Drizzle over the honey or maple syrup.
4. In a large mixing bowl, cream the butter and sugar until light and fluffy.
5. Beat in the eggs, one at a time, then the lemon juice.
6. Stir in the flour, baking powder, and baking soda. Pour the mixture over the apples and smooth the top.
7. Combine the brown sugar, lemon rind, and cinnamon. Sprinkle over the pudding.
8. Bake for 50–60 minutes, until a skewer inserted in the center comes out clean. Serve warm with English Custard Sauce (page 105) or heavy cream.

APPLE FOOL

PREPARATION TIME: 5 MINUTES   YIELD: 6–8 SERVINGS

1 cup heavy cream
2 tablespoons confectioners' sugar
2 cups apple sauce
½ teaspoon ground cinnamon

1. Pour the heavy cream into a medium-size bowl. Add the confectioners' sugar and beat until stiff.
2. Fold in the apple sauce.
3. Spoon into individual dessert dishes, if desired, and sprinkle the tops with a little cinnamon.

APPLE SORBET

PREPARATION TIME: 3 MINUTES, PLUS 2 HOURS FREEZING TIME   YIELD: 1 QUART

2 cups apple sauce
2 cups apple juice or cider
¼ cup honey
1 teaspoon ground ginger or
  ground cinnamon

1. Combine all the ingredients in a medium-size bowl, blender, or food processor, and blend together. Chill for 1 hour.
2. Pour into an ice cream machine and follow the manufacturer's directions for freezing ice cream. Or pour into a shallow dish and place in the freezer for about 1 hour. Then beat the mixture, cover with foil, and freeze until firm.

ENGLISH CUSTARD SAUCE

PREPARATION TIME: 10–15 MINUTES   YIELD: 2 CUPS

⅓ cup sugar
2 tablespoons cornstarch
3 large egg yolks
2 cups milk or light cream
1 tablespoon vanilla extract

Dinner in England is always followed by "pudding," the name given to any sweet dessert. Pies and baked puddings are always served with double (clotted) cream or a custard such as this one. You can also serve this sauce with baked apples and any of the crisps and cobblers.

1. Combine the sugar and cornstarch, and whisk together with the egg yolks in the top of a double boiler. Whisk until smooth.
2. Heat the milk in a medium-size saucepan. When it reaches a boil, pour half over the egg mixture, stirring constantly. Add the rest of the milk and the vanilla.
3. Place the top of the double boiler *over* simmering water (it must not touch the water) and, stirring all the time, cook for 2 minutes or until the mixture thickens and is smooth.
4. Remove from the heat and pour into a small jug. Serve immediately or cover with waxed paper to prevent a skin forming.
5. For a richer custard, whip ½ cup heavy cream until it is thick but not stiff and stir into the custard. Chill, if desired.

APPLE PIZZA

PREPARATION TIME: 25 MINUTES   BAKING TIME: 30 MINUTES   YIELD: 8 SERVINGS

Pastry for a single pie crust
(pages 125–128)
5 large apples (Northern Spy,
Winesap, Rome Beauty)
½ cup grated cheddar,
mozzarella, or Swiss cheese
½ cup chopped walnuts
½ cup dark brown sugar
½ teaspoon ground cinnamon
½ teaspoon ground nutmeg
2 tablespoons sweet butter or
margarine

1. Preheat the oven to 400°F. Grease a 12-inch pizza pan.
2. Roll the pastry into a 13-inch circle and place on the greased pizza pan. Form a rim around the edge.
3. Bake in the oven for 10 minutes.
4. Peel, core, and slice the apples into ¼-inch pieces. Arrange on the pizza crust and sprinkle with the grated cheese.
5. Mix together the walnuts, brown sugar, and spices. Sprinkle on top of the cheese.
6. Cut the butter into small pieces and dot over the top.
7. Bake for 20 minutes, or until the apples are tender. Serve hot.

APPLE DUMPLINGS I

PREPARATION TIME: 30 MINUTES   BAKING TIME: 45 MINUTES   YIELD: 6 SERVINGS

6 medium-size apples (Rome
Beauty, Granny Smith,
Jonathan)
¼ cup sweet butter or margarine,
softened
¼ cup apricot preserves
2 tablespoons brown sugar
Pastry for a double pie crust
(pages 125–128)
Milk

1. Preheat the oven to 400°F. Grease a large shallow baking dish.
2. Peel and core the apples three-quarters of the way down. Remove the stem and trim the bottoms, if necessary, to allow the apples stand level.
3. Beat the butter, apricot preserves, and brown sugar together. Stuff into the core of each apple.
4. Divide the pastry into 6 and roll out into 6-inch squares approximately ¼ inch thick.
5. Place an apple in the center of each square of dough and bring the 4 corners of the pastry together. Dab with milk and seal.
6. Arrange the dumplings on the greased baking dish (they should not touch) and pop in the freezer for 3-5 minutes to chill the pastry.
7. Brush with milk and bake for 45 minutes. Serve warm with English Custard (page 105) or heavy cream.

APPLE DUMPLINGS II

PREPARATION TIME: 30 MINUTES   BAKING TIME: 45 MINUTES   YIELD: 6 SERVINGS

6 large apples (Cortland,
  Winesap, Northern Spy)
Juice and grated rind of 1 lemon
¼ cup chopped walnuts
¾ cup pitted dates, chopped
2 tablespoons honey
2 teaspoons ground cinnamon
Pastry for a double pie crust
  (pages 125–128)

1. Preheat the oven to 400°F.
2. Peel and core the apples, leaving approximately ¼ inch of core at the base. Remove the stem and trim the bottoms if necessary so that the apples stand level.
3. Sprinkle each apple with lemon juice.
4. Mix together the walnuts, dates, honey, lemon rind, and cinnamon. Stuff into the core of each apple.
5. Divide the pastry into 6 and roll out into 6-inch squares approximately ¼ inch thick.
6. Place an apple in the center of each square of dough and bring the 4 corners of the pastry together. Dab with milk and seal.
7. Arrange the dumplings on a greased baking dish (they should not touch), and pop in the freezer for 3–5 minutes to chill the pastry.
8. Brush with milk and bake for 45 minutes. Serve warm with English Custard Sauce (page 105) or heavy cream.

CHEESE AND APPLE TARTLETS

PREPARATION TIME: 30 MINUTES   COOKING AND BAKING TIME: 30 MINUTES   YIELD: 12 SMALL TARTS

**Pastry for a single pie crust
(pages 125–128)**
**4 large apples (Granny Smith,
Rhode Island Greening)**
2–4 tablespoons sugar
½ teaspoon ground nutmeg
¾ cup grated cheddar cheese

1. Preheat the oven to 350°F. Grease 12 shallow muffin cups or a special tartlet tin tray.
2. Roll out the pastry to a rectangle ⅛ inch thick. Using a 3-inch round pastry cutter, cut out 12 circles and fit into the greased tartlet tins. Pat the pastry up the sides and around the rims of the molds and press down with fork tines.
3. Prick the base of each tiny crust with a fork and fill each with crumpled aluminum paper or dried beans. Bake for 15 minutes. Remove the aluminum paper or beans and return to the oven for 5 minutes. Remove and cool on a wire tray.
4. Peel, core, and slice the apples. Put into a saucepan, cover, and cook slowly until soft, approximately 20 minutes. Remove the lid and cook for 5–10 minutes longer, until the moisture has evaporated.
5. Add the sugar and nutmeg. Stir together until the mixture is like a thick puree. Cool.
6. Fill the cool tartlet crusts with the cool apple puree. Top with grated cheddar cheese and place under the broiler for 1 minute to melt the cheese. Serve warm or cooled.

APPLE TURNOVERS

PREPARATION TIME: 30 MINUTES   BAKING TIME: 30 MINUTES   YIELD: 8 TURNOVERS

4 medium-size apples (McIntosh, Golden Delicious)
1 tablespoon lemon juice
2 tablespoons sweet butter
⅓ cup sugar
1 tablespoon cornstarch
Pastry for a double pie crust (pages 125–128)
Milk

1. Grease a large cookie sheet.
2. Peel, core, and slice the apples into ¼-inch pieces. Place in a medium-size bowl. Sprinkle with the lemon juice.
3. Cut the butter into little pieces and add to the apple slices.
4. Mix the sugar and cornstarch together. Combine with the apple.
5. Divide the pastry into 8 equal parts and roll into 6-inch or 7-inch squares.
6. Spoon the filling onto the center of each square. Brush the edges with milk and fold over to make a triangle.
7. Press the edges together to seal and crimp with the tines of a fork. Using a sharp knife, make a steam vent in the middle of each. Place on the cookie sheet and refrigerate for 15 minutes.
8. Meanwhile, preheat the oven to 425°F.
9. Brush the turnovers with milk and bake for 30 minutes, or until golden brown. Remove from the baking sheet and serve warm or cold.

APPLE RAISIN TURNOVERS

PREPARATION TIME: 30 MINUTES   BAKING TIME: 30 MINUTES   YIELD: 8 TURNOVERS

4 medium-size apples
½ cup golden raisins
2 tablespoons apple juice or
  cider
½ cup sugar
1 teaspoon sugar
1 teaspoon ground cinnamon
Pastry for a double pie crust
  (pages 125–128)
Milk

1. Grease a large cookie sheet.
2. Peel, core, and slice the apples into ¼-inch pieces.
3. Place in a 2½-quart or 3-quart saucepan with the rest of the ingredients (except the pastry) and simmer for 5 minutes. Remove from the heat.
4. Divide the pastry into 8 equal parts and roll into 6-inch or 7-inch circles.
5. Spread 3 tablespoons of the filling on each circle, moisten the edges with milk, and fold the pastry in half.
6. Press the edges together to seal and crimp with the tines of a fork. Using a sharp knife, make a steam vent in the middle of each. Place on the cookie sheet and refrigerate for 15 minutes.
7. Meanwhile, preheat the oven to 425°F.
8. Brush the turnovers with milk and bake for 30 minutes, or until golden brown. Remove from the baking sheet and serve warm or cold.

LOUISE SALINGER'S APPLE PASTRY SQUARES

PREPARATION TIME: 35 MINUTES   BAKING TIME: 60 MINUTES   YIELD: 20 SERVINGS

2¾ cups presifted all-purpose
  flour
¾ cup sweet butter or margarine
1 large egg
¼ cup milk
8 medium-size apples
½ cup sugar
1 teaspoon ground cinnamon
1 cup cereal flakes (cornflakes,
  etc.)
Milk
1 cup confectioners' sugar
1 teaspoon vanilla extract
2 tablespoons water

1. Measure the flour into a medium-size bowl. Cut in the butter using 2 knives, a pastry blender, or food processor.
2. Beat the egg and ¼ cup milk together and mix with the flour mixture to form a firm dough. Divide into 2 pieces and refrigerate.
3. Preheat the oven to 400°F. Grease and flour a 15½-inch jelly roll pan.
4. Peel, core, and thinly slice the apples into a medium-size bowl. Mix with ½ cup sugar and the cinnamon.
5. Roll out half the dough to fit the bottom of the pan and sprinkle with the cereal flakes to within ½ inch of the edge.
6. Spoon the apple mixture on top of the flakes.
7. Roll out the remaining dough and place over the apples. Seal the edges by pinching together. Brush the pastry with a little milk.
8. Bake for 1 hour. Remove to a wire rack to cool.
9. While the pastry is still a little warm, combine the confectioners' sugar, vanilla extract, and water. Spread over the pastry. Serve warm or cold.

HARVEST APPLE PIE

PREPARATION TIME: 30 MINUTES   BAKING TIME: 50–60 MINUTES   YIELD: 8 SERVINGS

Pastry for a double 9-inch or
   10-inch pie crust (pages 125–128)
¼ cup melted apricot jam or
   marmalade
5 large apples (Idared, Jonathan,
   Rome Beauty)
2 tablespoons lemon juice
½ cup brown sugar, packed
2 tablespoons all-purpose flour
½ teaspoon cinnamon
¼ teaspoon nutmeg
1 tablespoon sweet butter
1½ teaspoons milk
1 teaspoon sugar

1. Preheat the oven to 400°F. Grease a 9-inch or 10-inch pie plate.
2. Roll out half of the pastry and fit it into the pie plate. Brush with the melted jam and refrigerate.
3. Peel, core, and cut the apple into ¼-inch slices. Place in a bowl and toss with the lemon juice.
4. Combine the brown sugar, flour, cinnamon, and nutmeg.
5. Layer half of the apple slices in the chilled crust and sprinkle with half of the sugar mixture. Repeat the layers. Cut the butter into small pieces and scatter over the apples.
6. Roll out the top crust, place over the filling, trim and flute the edges. Make 3 steam vents in the center.
7. Brush with the milk and sprinkle with the 1 teaspoon sugar.
8. Bake in middle of the oven for 50–60 minutes. If the crust edges brown too quickly, cover with strips of foil. Allow to cool for at least 10 minutes before serving.

PUMPKIN-APPLE PIE

PREPARATION TIME: 25 MINUTES   BAKING TIME: 50–55 MINUTES   YIELD: 8–10 SERVINGS

Pastry for a single 10-inch pie crust (pages 125–128)

2 medium-size apples (Rhode Island Greening, Newtown Pippin, Northern Spy) or 2 cups drained canned apple slices

1 teaspoon sweet butter

2 cups pumpkin puree, canned or fresh

2 large eggs

1 cup brown sugar

1½ cups light cream or half-and-half

1 teaspoon ground cinnamon

½ teaspoon ground nutmeg

¼ teaspoon ground cloves

¼ teaspoon ground ginger

1. Preheat the oven to 425°F. Grease a 10-inch pie plate.
2. Roll out the pastry and fit it into the pie plate. Trim and flute the edges. Refrigerate.
3. Peel, core, and slice the apples into ¼-inch pieces. Place in a skillet with 1 teaspoon butter, cover, and cook for 5 minutes. Remove from the heat and drain. If you are using canned apples, simply drain and set aside.
4. Place the remaining ingredients in a medium-size mixing bowl. Beat together until smooth.
5. Arrange the apple slices in the bottom of the chilled pastry shell and pour over the pumpkin mixture.
6. Bake in a 425°F. oven for 15 minutes. Reduce the heat to 375°F. and continue baking for 35–40 minutes, or until a knife inserted into the center comes out clean. Allow to cool before serving.

MOTHER'S APPLE AND BRAMBLE BERRY DEEP DISH PIE

PREPARATION TIME: 20 MINUTES   BAKING TIME: 40 MINUTES   YIELD: 8 SERVINGS

5 large apples (Rhode Island
   Greening, Granny Smith)
1½ cups blackberries or bramble
   berries
1 cup sugar
1 tablespoon apple juice or
   lemon juice
Pastry for a single pie crust
   (pages 125–128)
1 egg white

This is very juicy because no thickener is added. If you prefer the consistency to be thicker, mix 3 tablespoons flour with the sugar.

1. Preheat the oven to 400°F. Grease a 2-quart casserole or soufflé dish.
2. Peel, core, and cut the apples into ¼-inch slices. Layer half in the dish.
3. Sprinkle with half the sugar. Cover with the berries, then the rest of the sugar, finishing with the apple slices.
4. Roll out the pastry 1½ inches larger than the dish. Cover the filling with the pastry, turn under the overhang, trimming where necessary, and press firmly to the rim of the dish. Make a pattern, if desired, with fork tines.
5. Cut 3 steam vents in the crust and brush with a beaten egg white to glaze. Bake for 40 minutes or until the pastry is golden. If the pie edges start to brown too quickly, cover with aluminum foil. Allow the pie to cool and serve with English Custard Sauce (page 105).

APPLE AND RASPBERRY PIE

Pastry for a double pie crust (pages 125–128)
1 tablespoon raspberry jam
12-ounce package frozen raspberries
1½ tablespoons cornstarch
¼ cup sugar
¼ cup all-purpose flour
⅓ cup sugar
4 large apples (Rome Beauty)

1. Preheat the oven to 425°F. Grease a 9-inch or 10-inch pie plate.
2. Roll out half of the pastry and fit it into the pie plate. Smooth the raspberry jam over the bottom of the pie shell. Refrigerate
3. Thaw and drain the raspberries. Pour the juice into a small saucepan, stir in the cornstarch and ¼ cup sugar.
4. Bring the cornstarch mixture to a boil over low heat, stirring until the juice is thick and smooth. Remove from the heat, stir in the drained raspberries, and cool.
5. Combine the flour and the remaining ⅓ cup sugar.
6. Peel, core, and cut the apples into ¼-inch slices.
7. Alternate layers of apple slices and the flour mixture in the chilled pie shell. Top with the cooled raspberry mixture.
8. Roll out the top crust, place over the filling, trim and flute the edges. Make 3 steam slits in the center.
9. Bake at 425°F. for 15 minutes, reduce the heat to 350°F. and continue baking for 30–40 minutes, until the crust is golden brown. If the edges start getting too brown, cover with aluminum foil. Allow the pie to set before serving. Serve warm, with or without English Custard Sauce (page 105).

115

APPLE AND RAISIN DEEP DISH PIE

PREPARATION TIME: 30 MINUTES   BAKING TIME: 40 MINUTES   YIELD: 8–10 SERVINGS

5 large apples (Golden Delicious)
1–1½ cups raisins
1 tablespoon rum or applejack
2 tablespoons apple juice or
cider
Juice and grated rind of ½ lemon
½ cup brown sugar
½ teaspoon ground allspice
¼ teaspoon ground cloves
¼ teaspoon ground ginger
2 tablespoons all-purpose flour
Pastry for a single 9-inch pie
crust (pages 125–128)

1. Preheat the oven to 400°F. Grease a 2-quart soufflé or casserole dish.
2. Peel, core, and cut the apples into ¼-inch slices.
3. Toss the apple slices, raisins, rum, apple juice, lemon juice, and rind together in a large bowl.
4. Mix together the sugar, spices, and flour. Combine with the apple mixture. Turn into the greased dish.
5. Roll out the pastry 1½ inches larger than the dish. Place over the filling, turn under the overhang, trimming where necessary, and press firmly to seal the pastry against the rim of the dish. Make a pattern around the edges with fork tines.
6. Cut 3 steam vents in the crust (and brush with milk or beaten egg if a glaze is desired). Bake for 40 minutes or until the pastry is golden. If the crust edges start to brown too quickly, cover with strips of aluminum foil. Allow to cool before serving.

APPLE CRUMB PIE

PREPARATION TIME: 30 MINUTES   BAKING TIME: 55 MINUTES   YIELD: 8 SERVINGS

Pastry for a single 10-inch pie
  crust (pages 125–128)
5 large apples (Northern Spy,
  Rhode Island Greening)
1½ cups sour cream
1 large egg
1 tablespoon vanilla extract
¾ cup sugar
¼ cup all-purpose flour
½ cup all-purpose flour
½ cup dark brown sugar
½ cup sweet butter
1 cup chopped pecans

This recipe was given to me by Louise Salinger of Salinger's Orchard, Brewster, New York. After being married to an orchardist for 40 years and raising a family, Louise knows more about apples and pies than anyone else I've met. She is a superb cook and other recipes of hers are to be found elsewhere in this book.

1. Preheat the oven to 450°F. Grease a 10-inch pie plate.
2. Roll out the pastry and fit it into the pie plate. Flute the edges and refrigerate.
3. Peel, core, and slice the apples into ¼-inch pieces. Arrange in the chilled pie shell.
4. In a small bowl, combine the sour cream, egg, vanilla, sugar, and ¼ cup flour. Beat until smooth and pour over the apple slices.
5. Bake in a 450°F. oven for 10 minutes, reduce the heat to 350°F. and bake for another 30 minutes.
6. Mix the remaining ½ cup flour, the brown sugar and the butter together until the mixture is crumbly. Stir in the pecans and sprinkle over the baked pie.
7. Return the pie to the oven and continue baking for 15 minutes or until the topping is golden brown.

APPLE CRANBERRY MERINGUE PIE

Pastry for a single 9-inch pie
  crust (pages 125–128)
1 egg white
3 medium-size apples (Idared,
  Empire, Golden Delicious)
½ cup brown sugar
¼ cup all-purpose flour
½ teaspoon ground cinnamon
½ teaspoon ground ginger
2 cups fresh cranberries
½ cup sugar
3 large egg whites, at room
  temperature
¼ teaspoon cream of tartar
½ cup sugar

1. Preheat the oven to 425°F. Grease a 9-inch pie plate.
2. Roll out the pastry and fit it into the pie plate. Flute the edges.
3. Beat 1 egg white and brush it over the bottom pastry. Refrigerate.
4. Peel, core, and cut the apples into ¼-inch slices. Place in a medium-size bowl.
5. Mix together the brown sugar, flour, and spices. Toss with the apple slices and turn into the chilled crust.
6. Combine the cranberries and ½ cup sugar. Using a fork, lightly crush the cranberries. Spread over the apples.
7. Cover the filling with a piece of aluminum foil in which a ½-inch hole has been cut in the middle to act as a steam vent.
8. Place the pie in the oven and bake at 425°F. for 15 minutes. Reduce the heat to 350°F. and bake for another 45 minutes. Remove from the oven.
9. To make the meringue topping, place the 3 egg whites and cream of tartar in a medium-size bowl. Using electric beaters, whip until foamy. Gradually add the remaining ½ cup sugar—2 tablespoons at a time—beating during the entire process. When the whites are stiff, spread over the hot filling, bringing the meringue to the edge of the crust to form a seal. Return the pie to the oven to bake for 12–15 minutes at 350°F., until golden. Allow the pie to set for at least 30 minutes before serving.

HANK KEENAN'S PEACH AND APPLE DEEP DISH PIE

PREPARATION TIME: 30 MINUTES   BAKING TIME: 40 MINUTES   YIELD: 8–10 SERVINGS

5 medium-size apples (Cortland,
    Golden Delicious)
5 medium-size peaches
2 teaspoons grated lemon rind
¼ cup instant tapioca
¾ cup sugar
½ teaspoon ground cinnamon
½ teaspoon ground ginger
½ teaspoon nutmeg
Pastry for a single pie crust
    (pages 125–128)

Hank is a photographer who also sells apples at Salinger's Orchard in Brewster, New York. When I was buying apples and peaches one day at the end of summer, Hank described the apple and peach pie he'd made that weekend. It sounded so delicious that when I arrived home I reconstructed it—he didn't work from a recipe. I made one major change; I made it smaller. Hank had used 8 apples, 8 peaches, and the rind of a whole lemon.

1. Preheat the oven to 400°F. Grease a 2-quart casserole or soufflé dish.
2. Peel, core, and slice the apples into ¼-inch pieces. Put in a bowl.
3. Remove the stones from the peaches and slice into ½-inch pieces. Place in a separate bowl.
4. Mix the lemon rind, tapioca, sugar, and spices together.
5. Sprinkle the apple slices with the spice mixture and toss until completely coated.
6. Starting with the apple slices, layer the apples and peaches in the greased dish.
7. Roll out the pastry 1½ inches larger than the casserole. Cover the filling with the pastry, turn under the overhang, trimming where necessary, and press firmly to the rim of the dish. Make a pattern around the edges with fork tines, if desired.
8. Cut 3 steam vents in the crust and bake for 40 minutes or until the pastry is golden. If the pie edges start to brown too quickly, cover with aluminum foil. Allow the pie to cool before serving.

APPLE, RHUBARB, AND STRAWBERRY STREUSEL PIE

PREPARATION TIME: 30 MINUTES   BAKING TIME: 45 MINUTES   YIELD: 8 SERVINGS

2 cups rolled oats
½ cup light brown sugar
½ cup sweet butter or margarine,
   melted
¾ cup sugar
⅓ cup all-purpose flour
½ teaspoon ground ginger
¼ teaspoon ground nutmeg
2 medium-size apples (Rome
   Beauty)
2 cups sliced rhubarb stems
2 cups whole strawberries, hulled

1. Preheat the oven to 425°F. Grease a 10-inch pie plate.
2. In a medium-size bowl, combine the oats, brown sugar, and melted butter. Blend well.
3. Take two-thirds of this mixture and press firmly onto the bottom and up the sides of the pie plate. Refrigerate.
4. Mix together ¾ cup sugar, the flour, and spices in a large bowl.
5. Peel, core, and slice the apples into ¼-inch pieces.
6. Toss the apples, rhubarb, and strawberries with the spiced sugar and flour and turn into the chilled streusel base. Sprinkle with the remaining streusel crumbs.
7. Bake at 425°F. for 15 minutes. Reduce the heat to 375°F. and continue baking for 30 minutes or until golden brown. Allow to cool before serving.

APPLE SAUCE TART

PREPARATION TIME: 25 MINUTES   BAKING TIME: 45 MINUTES   YIELD: 6–8 SERVINGS

Pastry for a single 9-inch pie
   crust (pages 125–128)
3 cups unsweetened apple sauce
3 large eggs, at room
   temperature, separated
2 tablespoons butter
½ cup brown sugar
1 teaspoon ground cinnamon
2 tablespoons orange juice
2 teaspoons grated orange rind
½ cup sugar

1. Preheat the oven to 400°F. Grease a 9-inch pie plate.
2. Roll out the pastry, line the pie plate, and flute the edges. Refrigerate.
3. Heat the apple sauce in a 2-quart saucepan and remove from the heat.
4. Beat in the egg yolks, butter, brown sugar, cinnamon, orange juice, and orange rind. Beat until well combined. Set aside.
5. In a medium-size bowl, whip the egg whites until foamy, using electric beaters. Then beat in ½ cup sugar, a little at a time. When the whites stand in stiff peaks, fold them into the apple sauce mixture.
6. Turn into the pie shell and bake at 400°F. for 15 minutes. Reduce the heat to 325°F. and continue baking for 30 minutes. Allow the tart to cool before serving.

APPLE CREAM CHEESE TART

PREPARATION TIME: 45 MINUTES   BAKING TIME: 55–60 MINUTES   YIELD: 10–12 SERVINGS

½ cup sweet butter
¼ cup sugar
1 teaspoon lemon juice
1 cup presifted all-purpose flour
1 pound cream cheese
½ cup brown sugar
1 large egg
1 tablespoon vanilla extract
2 large apples (Cortland, Rome
   Beauty)
½ cup sugar
1 teaspoon ground cinnamon

1. Cream the butter, ¼ cup sugar, and lemon juice together in a large bowl.
2. Stir in the flour until well blended.
3. Press the dough onto the bottom and about 1½ inches up the sides of a 9-inch springform pan. Refrigerate.
4. Preheat the oven to 425°F.
5. Place the cream cheese and brown sugar in a mixing bowl, and beat until fluffy.
6. Add the egg and vanilla. Beat until smooth.
7. Peel, core, and slice the apples into ¼-inch pieces.
8. In a large bowl, combine the remaining ½ cup sugar and cinnamon. Add the apple slices and toss until coated.
9. Pour the cream cheese filling into the prepared crust and cover with the sugared apple slices.
10. Bake for 15 minutes at 425°F., reduce the heat to 350°F., and continue baking for 40–45 minutes.
11. Remove from the oven and cool on a wire rack. Use a knife to loosen the cake before releasing the spring and lifting the sides from the bottom of the pan.

FRENCH APPLE TART

PREPARATION TIME: 30 MINUTES   BAKING TIME: 45 MINUTES   YIELD: 8 SERVINGS

Pastry for a single 10-inch pie
   crust (page 125–128)
1 beaten egg white
10 large apples (Mutsu,
   Winesap, Jonagold or 14–15
   Golden Delicious)
2 tablespoons lemon juice
2 tablespoons sugar
2 tablespoons sweet butter
½ cup brown sugar
¼ cup orange, lemon, or apple
   marmalade
2 tablespoons brandy (optional)
¼ cup apple jelly or marmalade

1. Preheat the oven to 400°F. Grease a 10-inch pie plate or flan tin.
2. Roll out the pastry and fit it into the pie plate. Flute the edges, brush the bottom with the beaten egg white, and refrigerate.
3. Peel, core, and slice the apples into ½-inch pieces. Place half the apples in a 3-quart or 4 quart saucepan (don't overcrowd the apples or it will take longer for the juice to evaporate). Place the remainder in a medium-size bowl. Toss those in the bowl with the 2 tablespoons lemon juice and 2 tablespoons sugar.
4. To the apple slices in the saucepan, add the butter, brown sugar, ¼ cup marmalade, and brandy. Cover the pan and cook over low heat for 15 minutes. Remove the cover, beat the mixture, and cook for another 5–10 minutes. The mixture should be thick and smooth. Remove from the heat and cool.
5. When the apple sauce has cooled slightly, turn it into the chilled pie shell and arrange the tossed apple slices decoratively on top. Bake in the 400°F. oven for 15 minutes. Reduce the heat to 350°F. and continue baking for another 30 minutes.
6. Melt the remaining ¼ cup apple jelly or marmalade and brush over the baked apple slices. Allow to cool slightly before serving.

SHERRIED APPLE CRÊPES

PREPARATION TIME: 65 MINUTES   YIELD: 8 SERVINGS

4 small apples (McIntosh,
  Golden Delicious)
1 tablespoon apple juice or water
¼ cup sugar
½ teaspoon ground cinnamon
½ teaspoon ground nutmeg
3 tablespoons golden raisins
2 tablespoons slivered blanched
  almonds
¼ cup apricot jam
8 crêpes (page 124)
1 cup heavy cream
2 tablespoons confectioners'
  sugar
1 tablespoon sherry

1. Peel, core, and thinly slice the apples. Place in a pan with the apple juice, sugar, cinnamon, nutmeg, raisins, almonds, and apricot jam. Mix together.
2. Simmer gently, stirring occasionally, for 10–15 minutes, or until the apples are soft and the mixture thick. Allow to cool.
3. Make the crêpes following the basic recipe on page 124.
4. Whip the heavy cream until thickened, stir in the confectioners' sugar and sherry, and continue beating until soft peaks form.
5. Fold half of the whipped cream into the apple mixture. Spread the filling over the pancakes, fold in half, then in half again to form triangles. Top each pancake with a spoonful of reserved whipped cream.

APPLE ENVELOPE

PREPARATION TIME: 15 MINUTES   BAKING TIME: 45 MINUTES   YIELD: 2 SERVINGS

3 medium-size apples (McIntosh)
2 tablespoons honey
1 teaspoon ground allspice
¼ cup raisins
Pastry for a single 9-inch pie
   crust (pages 125–128)
Milk
Sugar

1. Preheat the oven to 400°F.
2. Peel, core, and slice the apples into ¼-inch pieces.
3. In a medium-size bowl, combine the apples with the honey, allspice, and raisins.
4. Roll out the pastry to a circle approximately 10 inches in diameter. Use a 10-inch plate as a guide, if possible.
5. Spoon the apple mixture over half the dough, leaving a 1-inch border. Fold the other half over the apples, moisten the edges with milk, and seal. Crimp the edges with fork tines or a fork handle.
6. Place on a greased baking pan, brush with milk, and sprinkle with sugar.
7. Bake for 45 minutes. Serve warm with English Custard Sauce (page 105) or heavy cream.

BASIC CRÊPE RECIPE

PREPARATION TIME: 10 MINUTES   COOKING TIME: 3 MINUTES PER PANCAKE   YIELD: 8–10 CRÊPES

1 cup milk
¼ cup water or apple juice
2 large eggs
2 tablespoons vegetable oil or
   melted shortening
1 cup presifted all-purpose flour
2 tablespoons sugar (optional)
1 tablespoon vanilla extract
   (optional)

1. Combine all the ingredients in a blender or mixing bowl and beat until smooth. The sugar and vanilla should be added if you are making dessert crêpes.
2. Heat an 8-inch skillet over medium heat and add a small pat of butter.
3. Pour a ¼ cup of batter into the skillet and tilt until the batter covers the bottom. Cook for 1 minute or so, or until the crêpe is golden brown underneath. Turn with a spatula and cook for 1–2 minutes.
4. Repeat with the rest of the batter. Stack the crêpes between waxed paper on a plate and keep warm in a low oven, or serve each one immediately.

FLAKY PASTRY

PREPARATION TIME: 5–10 MINUTES, PLUS 30 MINUTES CHILLING TIME   YIELD: TWO 10-INCH PIE CRUSTS, 8 DUMPLINGS, OR TWELVE 6-INCH TURNOVERS

3 cups presifted all-purpose flour
1 cup vegetable shortening or
   lard
3 tablespoons sugar (for sweet
   pastry)
½ cup ice-cold water

Although not as flavorful as a crust made with butter, the tenderest pastry is made with solid vegetable shortening or lard.

1. Sift the flour into a medium-size bowl. Cut in the shortening with 2 knives, a pastry blender, or in a food processor, until the mixture resembles coarse crumbs. (Add the sugar, if desired.)
2. Using a fork, stir in the water, a tablespoon at a time, until the dough forms a ball. Too much water or overmixing will make the crust tough.
3. Divide the dough into 2 pieces and flatten into 6-inch circles. Wrap in waxed paper and refrigerate for 30 minutes.
4. Roll out the pastry to a 12-inch circle, about ⅛ inch thick. Loosely fold the circle in half, fit into a buttered pie plate (butter browns and crisps the pastry more than shortening), and trim, leaving a 1-inch overhang.
5. Brush the crust with a beaten egg white or jam or jelly to help prevent the bottom from becoming soggy. If the jam is too solid or cold to spread, melt it first, but cool before brushing onto the pastry. Refrigerate until the filling is ready.
6. Roll out the second piece of dough. Carefully lift the pastry and place over the filling. Trim if necessary. Seal to the bottom crust. Flute the edges, cut 2 or 3 steam vents in the center, and brush with a beaten egg or milk. Sprinkle with sugar if desired. Bake according to the recipe directions.

SHORT PASTRY

PREPARATION TIME: 5–10 MINUTES, PLUS 30 MINUTES CHILLING TIME   YIELD: TWO 9-INCH PIE CRUSTS, 6 DUMPLINGS, OR EIGHT TO TEN 6-INCH TURNOVERS

2½ cups presifted all-purpose flour
6 tablespoons solid vegetable shortening or lard
6 tablespoons sweet butter
2 tablespoons sugar (for sweet pastry)
6 tablespoons ice-cold water

1. Sift the flour into a medium-size bowl. Cut in the shortening and butter with 2 knives, a pastry blender, or in a food processor, until the mixture resembles coarse crumbs. (Add the sugar, if desired.)
2. Using a fork, stir in the water, a tablespoon at a time, until the dough forms a ball. Too much water or overmixing will make the crust tough.
3. Divide the dough into 2 pieces and flatten into 6-inch circles. Wrap in waxed paper and refrigerate for 30 minutes.
4. Roll out the pastry to a 12-inch circle, about ⅛ inch thick. Loosely fold the circle in half, fit into a buttered pie plate, and trim, leaving a 1-inch overhang.
5. Brush the crust with a beaten egg white or jam or jelly to help prevent the bottom from becoming soggy. If the jam is too solid or cold to spread, melt it first, but cool before brushing onto the pastry. Refrigerate until the filling is ready.
6. Roll out the second piece of dough. Carefully lift the pastry and place over the filling. Trim if necessary. Seal to the bottom crust. Flute the edges, cut 2 or 3 steam vents in the center, and brush with beaten egg or milk. Sprinkle with sugar if desired. Bake according to the recipe directions.

CHEESE PASTRY

PREPARATION TIME: 5–10 MINUTES, PLUS 30 MINUTES CHILLING TIME   YIELD: TWO 9-INCH PIE CRUSTS, 6 DUMPLINGS, OR EIGHT TO TEN 6-INCH TURNOVERS

2½ cups presifted all-purpose flour
¾ cup solid vegetable shortening
½ cup grated cheddar cheese
⅓–½ cup ice cold water

Use this pastry for a change when making a plain apple pie, apple turnovers, or dumplings.

1. Sift the flour into a medium-size bowl and cut in the shortening with 2 knives or a pastry blender until coarse crumbs form. Stir in the grated cheese with a fork.
2. Using a fork, stir in the water, a tablespoon at a time, until the dough forms a ball. Too much water or overmixing will make the crust tough.
3. Divide the dough into 2 pieces and flatten into 6-inch circles. Wrap in waxed paper and refrigerate for 30 minutes.
4. Roll out the pastry to a 12-inch circle, about ⅛ inch thick. Loosely fold the circle in half, fit into a buttered pie plate, and trim, leaving a 1-inch overhang.
5. Brush the crust with a beaten egg white or jam or jelly to help prevent the bottom from becoming soggy. If the jam is too solid or cold to spread, melt it first, but cool before brushing onto the pastry. Refrigerate until the filling is ready.
6. Roll out the second piece of dough. Carefully lift the pastry and place over the filling. Trim if necessary. Seal to the bottom crust. Flute the edges, cut 2 or 3 steam vents in the center, and brush with beaten egg or milk. Sprinkle with sugar if desired. Bake according to the recipe directions.

BUTTER PIE CRUST

PREPARATION TIME: 5–10 MINUTES, PLUS 30 MINUTES CHILLING TIME   YIELD: 1 CRUST OR 12 SMALL TART SHELLS

1½ cups presifted all-purpose
   flour
½ cup sweet butter
1 tablespoon sugar (optional)
1 teaspoon lemon juice
¼ cup ice-cold water

1. Sift the flour into a medium-size bowl and cut in the butter with 2 knives, a pastry blender, or in a food processor. Mix in the sugar if desired.
2. Using a fork, stir in the lemon juice and water, 1 tablespoon at a time. When a ball forms, stop adding water, flatten, wrap in waxed paper, and refrigerate for 30 minutes.
3. Roll the pastry on a floured surface to a 12-inch circle, fold in half, and fit into the pie dish.
4. Trim so that a 1-inch overhang remains, turn under, pinch, and flute. Refrigerate until ready to use.
5. To bake an unfilled pie shell, prick the bottom and sides of the pastry with a fork to allow air to escape during baking. Bake in a preheated 450°F. oven for 10 minutes (prebaked), or 20 minutes (fully baked).

Variation: *WHOLE WHEAT CRUST*

If a whole wheat crust is desired, substitute ⅓ cup whole wheat flour for ½ cup all-purpose flour, and add a drop *more water if necessary.*

SMALL QUANTITY APPLE SAUCE

PREPARATION TIME: 15 MINUTES   COOKING TIME: 30 MINUTES   YIELD: ABOUT 5 CUPS

10 medium-size apples
1 tablespoon water, apple juice,
  or lemon juice
1 teaspoon ground nutmeg

This unsweetened apple sauce lends itself to any number of flavor additions, which make it a good accompaniment for savory dishes. For example, to serve with beef, add ½ cup of freshly grated horseradish to 2 cups of apple sauce. If pork or chicken is the main dish, add the grated rind of a lime and 2 tablespoons of honey to 2 cups of apple sauce. Stir in ½ teaspoon each of ground ginger and curry powder. Apple sauce to be served with duck or goose will be particularly tasty with the addition of 2 tablespoons of brandy and 2 tablespoons of honey to 2 cups of apple sauce.

1. Peel, core, and quarter the apples. Place in a large saucepan with the liquid and the nutmeg.
2. Cover the pot and simmer for approximately 30 minutes, until the apples are tender. Mash with a fork or puree in a blender or food processor to the desired consistency.

Note: For added flavor, leave the peel on and force the cooked apples through a sieve or food mill to separate the skins from the fruit.

SWEET APPLE SAUCE

PREPARATION TIME: 15 MINUTES   COOKING TIME: 30 MINUTES   YIELD: ABOUT 5½ CUPS

10 medium-size apples
3 tablespoons apple juice or
  cider
⅓ cup honey or ½ cup brown
  sugar or ½ cup apricot
  preserves
3 tablespoons sweet butter
½ teaspoon ground ginger
½ teaspoon ground cinnamon

1. Peel, core, and quarter the apples. Place in a large saucepan with the apple juice.
2. Cover the pot and simmer for approximately 30 minutes, or until the apples are tender. Puree in a blender or food processor.
3. Stir the honey, butter, and spices into the warm apple puree. Adjust sweetness and spices.

Note: The peels can be left on for added flavor. Cook the apples, then force them through a sieve or food mill to separate the skins from the fruit.

PRESERVING THE APPLE HARVEST

I f you've been harvesting apples since August, by the time the end of October rolls around, your family may wish it was a forbidden fruit. This is the time to start preserving.

There are a number of ways to prolong the life of your apples: canning, freezing, drying, and root cellaring. Apple sauce and apple slices are a cinch to can or freeze. You may decide to make jams, jellies, and butters, or, on the savory side, to try your hand at spicy chutneys and relishes.

If apple pies are a staple in your house, unbaked pies can be frozen and later popped, at a moment's notice, from the freezer into a 425°F. oven for about 1 hour. I don't like to freeze baked pies; the bottom crust always ends up soggy.

Drying is another good way to preserve apple slices for later use as snacks, pie fillings, and other baked apple dishes. If there are children in your house, no doubt you'll want to make dried fruit roll-ups (otherwise known as leathers) for apple snacks.

soften quite rapidly; they ripen as much in one day at 70°F. as they will in 10 days at 40°F. Unfortunately, most home root cellars are too warm in the early fall to provide sufficiently cool temperatures for optimum storage conditions. Still, in an insulated root cellar or unheated basement, you can keep apples in bins for a month or two. Check regularly and remove any that are rotting. If the apples show signs of deteriorating, make apple sauce to prevent waste. If possible, keep the cellar open to the cool night air to keep the cellar chilled.

CANNING VS. FREEZING

Canning and freezing provide long-term storage for apples. Frozen apples will keep for 8–12 months in a freezer before they deteriorate in flavor and texture, especially if they are packed in a sugar or honey syrup. Canned apples and apple sauce will keep indefinitely, although it is always best to can only as much as you can eat in a year.

Most people find that they don't have much room in their freezer for frozen apple sauce or slices, so they prefer to can apples. I prefer to can apple slices and apple sauces, because I like the convenience of having the foods ready to eat or bake with right out of the jar. Frozen apple sauce takes quite a long time to defrost.

ROOT CELLARING

You are among the lucky few if you are able to provide ideal storage conditions for apples. The ideal storage temperature for apples is 32–34°F., conditions commercial growers are capable of producing. At temperatures above 32°F., apples ripen and

CANNING BASICS

Apple slices, apple sauce, and apple preserves can be canned in a boiling water bath, which consists of a large kettle, a rack that fits within, and a lid. The filled jars are placed in the hot (not boiling) water. More water is added, if necessary, to cover the jars by 1–2 inches. The water is brought to a boil, then you begin to count the processing time, according to the recipe instructions. Apple slices are usually processed for 15 minutes in pints, 20 minutes in quarts. Apple sauce is processed for 10 minutes in pints or quarts. It is a good idea to process apple jams and marmalades for 10 minutes to ensure a long shelf life.

Whenever you can fruits or vegetables, you should use special canning jars, which are equipped with either flat metal lids and screw bands, or have glass lids with a separate rubber seal and metal clamp.

A jar lifter and a wide-necked funnel will make the canning process a lot easier, safer, and, in the case of the funnel, a lot neater.

When using metal canning lids, after the jars have cooled for 12 hours, check each one for a proper seal by feeling the depression on the lid. When canning with jars with glass lids, stretch a new rubber ring to fit the ledge near the rim of the jar. Wipe off any fruit or syrup before fitting the glass lid on top of the rubber ring. Leave the short wire up to process. After removing from the boiling water bath, push the short wire down to create a seal. If you find a jar—with either a glass top or a metal lid—that hasn't sealed

(check by turning it upside down to see if it leaks), take a clean jar and a new lid, fill with the mixture, and reprocess for the given time, or refrigerate that jar and use within a week or so. Reprocessing apple sauce will not affect the texture significantly. Don't bother to reprocess apple slices, however, you will end up with apple sauce instead of slices.

CANNING APPLE SLICES

Canned apple slices are great to use in pies, crêpes, and baked desserts. They are good in fruit salads. However, peeling apples for canning is a laborious chore. When I am working with large quantities of apples, I prefer to can apple sauce. Plan to can about 3 medium-size apples per quart jar.

1. Wash the jars and lids in warm, soapy water and rinse clean. Prepare the lids according to the manufacturer's directions. Preheat water in your canner.

2. For each quart jar, measure out 2 cups of water and 1 cup extra fine granulated sugar into a pan and slowly bring to a boil, stirring to dissolve the sugar. Boil for 5 minutes and remove from the heat.

3. Peel, core, and slice the apples approximately ¼ inch thick. Drop immediately into a bowl containing a gallon of cold water mixed with 2 tablespoons of lemon juice.

4. When all the apples are sliced, drain and pack into the quart jars to within ½ inch of the top, without crushing the slices.

5. Return the syrup to a rolling boil and pour over the packed slices, again leaving ½ inch head room. Run a rubber spatula or chopstick around the inside of the jars to release air bubbles. Wipe the rim of the jar with a clean, damp cloth, and screw on the lids.

6. Place the jars in a boiling water bath without touching each other or the sides of the pan. Pour in hot water to cover the jars by 1–2 inches, cover the kettle, and bring the water to a boil. Process quart jars for 20 minutes (pints for 15 minutes) after the water comes to a boil.

7. Remove the jars and adjust the screw bands to tighten the seals. If you are using glass-top jars, clamp down the second wire.

8. Leave the jars undisturbed for 12 hours to cool. Test the seals. Store in a cool, dry place.

3. When the apples are soft, press through a sieve, strainer, or food mill to remove the skins and seeds.

4. Return the apple sauce to a kettle and bring to a boil. Cook for at least 10 minutes, or until the sauce reaches the desired consistency. Season to taste with sugar and cinnamon, if desired.

5. Ladle the hot apple sauce into hot, clean jars, leaving ½ inch head room. Wipe the rims with a clean, damp cloth, and screw on the lids.

6. Place the jars in a boiling water bath without touching each other or the sides of the pan. Pour in hot water to cover the jars by 1–2 inches. Cover the kettle and bring the water to a boil. Process pint and quart jars for 10 minutes after the water comes to a boil.

7. Remove the jars. Adjust the screw bands to tighten the seals. If you are using glass-top jars, clamp down the second wire.

8. Leave the jars undisturbed for 12 hours to cool. Test the seals. Store in a cool, dry place.

CANNING APPLE SAUCE

1. Figure that 1 bushel of apples (42 pounds) will give you 16–20 quarts of apple sauce. Wash and quarter the apples. It is not necessary to peel them. Place the apples in a kettle with about 1 inch of water. Cover and cook until soft, stirring occasionally to prevent scorching and to allow the apples to cook evenly.

2. While the apples cook, prepare your jars and lids, and preheat water in your canner. Wash the jars and lids in warm, soapy water; rinse. Prepare the lids according to the manufacturer's directions.

FREEZING APPLES

Even if you select only firm, fresh, and flavorful apples for freezing, you will find that the apples will soften and lose flavor during frozen storage. For this reason it is important to choose only perfect apples and to refer to the table on page 9 to see which varieties are recommended for freezing. When cooked apple sauce is to be frozen, choose those apples listed on the chart under the heading Sauce. Cooking protects the texture and flavor—as long as the sauce is used within a reasonable time.

Try to speed up the freezing process by placing the containers of just-packed fruit next to a freezing surface and leaving space around each one. When the containers of fruit are completely frozen, repack your freezer to its fullest advantage.

Following are three methods for freezing apple slices. The first method may be considered the simplest way of freezing slices; however, the flavor of those slices deteriorates faster than the apple slices prepared in Method Two. The hot syrup method seems to help the texture and flavor to last longer. I prefer the third method because no sugar is used, and this allows the apple slices to be used in both savory and sweet dishes.

Freezing Apple Slices: Method One

1. Peel, core, and cut 3 pounds apples (9 medium-size apples) into ¼ inch slices.
2. Drop the slices immediately into 1 gallon of cold water containing 2 tablespoons lemon juice to prevent discoloration. Remove after 5 minutes and drain. Instead of lemon juice, 1 teaspoon ascorbic acid powder can be used.
3. Sprinkle a layer of extra fine granulated sugar on a baking sheet and cover with a layer of apple slices. Continue layering and sprinkling until all the slices are coated with sugar. Pack gently into freezer containers (including all the sugar), leaving ½-inch head space, seal, and label.

Yield: 3 quarts

Freezing Apple Slices: Method Two

1. Peel, core, and cut 3 pounds apples (9 medium-size apples) into ¼-inch slices.
2. Drop immediately in a bowl containing 1 gallon cold water mixed with 2 tablespoons of lemon juice.
3. Combine 4 cups extra fine granulated sugar and 2 quarts water in a saucepan and slowly bring to a boil, stirring to dissolve the sugar. Bring to a rolling boil for 5 minutes. If desired, add 1 teaspoon powdered ascorbic acid to the syrup to prevent the apples from browning in the freezer.
4. Meanwhile, drain the apple slices and pack into the freezer containers, leaving a ½-inch head space.
5. Pour the boiling syrup over the apple slices, again leaving a ½-inch head space. Cover the containers, label, and freeze.
6. Use in pies as you would freshly sliced apples; but first, thaw partially and drain.

Yield: 3 quarts

Freezing Apple Slices: Method Three

1. Peel, core, and slice 3 pounds apples (9 medium-size apples) into ¼-inch slices.
2. Drop into 1 gallon of water mixed with 2 tablespoons lemon juice.
3. Bring a pot of water to boiling and drop in the apple slices, a pound at a time. Blanch for 1 minute only. Drain immediately.
4. Place in single layers on baking trays and freeze.
5. When frozen, place in plastic freezer bags, seal and freeze.

Yield: 3 quarts

Freezing Whole Apples

1. Peel and core or wash and core the apples.
2. Drop into a pot of boiling water and blanch for 1 minute.
3. Drain and stuff with a mixture of nuts and raisins bound together with honey.
4. Wrap individually in plastic wrap or waxed paper. Place in freezer bags and put into the freezer.
5. To prepare the apples for the table, remove from the freezer and place in a buttered dish, dot with butter, cover, and bake in a 400°F. preheated oven for 30 minutes, or until they can be pierced easily with a fork.

Freezing Pies

If you intend to freeze baked pies, make sure they are completely cold before enclosing them in freezer bags. Any heat left in the pie results in condensation in the freezer bag, which causes the pie to become moist and the crust soggy.

Bake frozen in a preheated 375°F. oven for approximately 30 minutes. Cover the top with aluminum foil if the crust gets too brown.

Unbaked pies can be assembled as usual, but don't put steam vents in the top crust until you are ready to bake. Bake frozen in a preheated 425°F. oven for 30 minutes. Reduce the heat to 375°F. and continue baking for 30–40 minutes longer. Cover the crust with aluminum foil if it gets too brown before the pie has finished baking.

MAKING JAMS, JELLIES, BUTTERS, AND CHUTNEYS

Making preserves is simple, economical, and wonderfully satisfying. I get infinite pleasure from surveying jars of golden apple butters, chunky marmalades and chutneys. And the clear, vivid green of mint apple jelly is a cause for admiration.

These homemade money-savers taste equally good on toast, or when accompanying a savory dish of curried chicken.

Of all fruits, tart cooking apples are in a class of their own for jam making because their high pectin content acts as a natural setting agent.

Just for safety, the USDA recommends that all jams, marmalades, butters, chutneys, and relishes be processed for 10 minutes in a boiling water bath. Jellies may be sealed by packing hot into hot, sterilized, 2-piece canning jars leaving only ⅛ inch head room, or by sealing with paraffin. When sealing with paraffin, leave ¼ inch head room. Cover the hot jelly with a ⅛-inch layer of hot paraffin. Don't pour more than ⅛ inch paraffin. A too-thick layer of paraffin may fail to seal. It is a good idea to prick any air bubbles on the surface of the paraffin with a sterilized needle.

Sterilizing Jars and Lids

1. Choose a pan that can be fitted with a false bottom (such as a plate) to prevent the jars from touching the bottom of the pan and cracking and deep enough to allow the water to cover the jars.

2. Wash the jars and lids in warm water containing a little dishwashing liquid. Rinse thoroughly.

3. Place the jars upright in the water bath and fill with hot (not boiling) water. Continue to fill the water bath until the jars are completely covered by water. Bring to a boil and continue to boil gently for 15 minutes. (Some dishwashers have a sterilizing cycle you can use to sterilize jars.)

4. Scald or boil the lids according to the manufacturer's instructions only.

5. As the jars are needed for filling, removed from the boiling water (or dishwasher) one at a time.

JOYSE'S BLACKBERRY AND APPLE JAM

PREPARATION TIME: 60 MINUTES   YIELD: ABOUT 4 PINTS

3 medium-size tart green apples (Granny Smith, Rhode Island Greening, Twenty Ounce)
½ cup water
6 cups blackberries
½ cup water
8 cups fine granulated sugar (4 pounds)

Breakfast at my mother's home would not be complete without a dish of this jam to accompany the toast.

1. Peel, core, and slice the apples. Reserve the parings. Place the slices in a large kettle with ½ cup water. Cover and simmer for 15–20 minutes, until the apples are soft.
2. Place the blackberries in a medium-size pan and add the apple parings tied in cheesecloth, and ½ cup of water. Simmer for 15–20 minutes until the fruit is soft.
3. Discard the apple parings. Add the blackberries and their liquid to the apples. (If a seedless jam is preferred, force the cooked blackberries through a sieve to remove the seeds, then add the fruit pulp to the apples.)
4. Stir in the sugar and dissolve over a very low heat.
5. Stir the fruit and bring to a rolling boil for approximately 10 minutes or until the jam sets when dropped onto a chilled saucer.
6. When a set has been reached, ladle the jam into 4 hot, clean pint-size jars. Leave ¼ inch head space, wipe the rim, and cap each jar immediately. Process for 10 minutes in a boiling water bath.

APPLE BUTTER

PREPARATION TIME: 45 MINUTES   COOKING TIME: ½ HOURS   YIELD: 2 PINTS

8–9 medium-size apples
  (Paulared, Golden Delicious,
  Empire, Idared, McIntosh)
1 teaspoon water
1 pound light brown sugar
1 orange

1. Core and quarter the apples. Place in a large pan, add 1 teaspoon of water, cover, and simmer on low for 30 minutes or until soft. Turn the apples halfway through the cooking time.
2. Grate the skin of the orange and reserve in a bowl. Cut the orange in half and squeeze the juice into the rind. You should have ½–¾ cup juice.
3. Press the cooked apples through a sieve. Discard the skins, return the pulp to the pan and stir in the brown sugar, the grated rind, and the juice of the orange.
4. Simmer over very low heat, stirring frequently, until the mixture is thick—about 1½ hours. (Or, pour the mixture into a roasting pan and bake uncovered at 350°F. for 1 hour, stirring occasionally. Reduce the oven to 250°F. and continue baking for another 2–3 hours or until thick.)
5. Remove from the heat and ladle into 2 hot, sterilized pint-size jars. Leave ¼ inch head space and cap each jar immediately. Process for 10 minutes in a boiling water bath.

RHUBARB-APPLE CHUTNEY

PREPARATION TIME: 30 MINUTES   COOKING TIME: 2 HOURS   YIELD: 7–8 PINTS

5 medium-size apples (Twenty Ounce, Granny Smith, Tydeman, Wellington)
4 pounds rhubarb stems, cut in 1-inch pieces
4 medium-size onions, chopped
1 pound dark raisins
1 pound dark brown sugar
2½ cups malt vinegar
¼ teaspoon cayenne
2 teaspoons curry powder
½ teaspoon ground cinnamon
½ teaspoon ground ginger
½ teaspoon ground mace
½ teaspoon ground cloves

This is delicious enough to eat by itself on whole wheat bread.

1. Peel, core, and coarsely chop the apples.
2. Place all ingredients in a large kettle, cover, and bring to a boil.
3. Remove the cover, reduce the heat to very low, and simmer, stirring occasionally, for about 2 hours, or until the mixture is thick and tender.
4. Ladle into 7–8 hot, sterilized pint-size jars, leaving ¼ inch head space, and cap each jar immediately. Process for 10 minutes in a boiling water bath.

APPLE-PEACH CHUTNEY

PREPARATION TIME: 30 MINUTES   COOKING TIME: 2 HOURS   YIELD: 7–8 PINTS

16 medium-size peaches (about 3 pounds)
8 medium-size apples (Puritan, Tydeman, Granny Smith)
1 large onion, chopped
1 pound light brown sugar
1 pound golden raisins
2 cups cider vinegar
1 tablespoon ground ginger
1½ teaspoons ground cinnamon
1 teaspoon ground nutmeg
½ teaspoon ground cloves

1. Peel, pit, and dice the peaches.
2. Peel, core, and dice the apples.
3. Combine all the ingredients in a large kettle, cover, and bring to a boil.
4. Remove the cover, reduce the heat to very low, and simmer for approximately 2 hours, until the chutney is thick and tender. Ladle into 7–8 hot, sterilized pint-size jars, leaving ¼ inch head space, and cap each one immediately. Process for 10 minutes in a boiling water bath.

CANNED (PICKLED) CRAB APPLES

3 pounds crab apples
3 cups extra fine granulated
  sugar or 2½ cups honey
2½ cups cider vinegar
2½ cups water
1 teaspoon whole cloves
1 teaspoon whole cardamom
  seeds
3 sticks cinnamon, each broken
  in 2 or 3 pieces

1. Wash the crab apples (discard those that are blemished), wipe clean the blossom ends, and leave the stem intact but trimmed short.
2. Prick the crab apples in 2 or 3 places with a fine skewer and place half in a large kettle. Cover with the sugar (or honey), vinegar, and water. Stir all together.
3. Tie the spices in cheesecloth and add to the crab apples in the kettle.
4. Cover the kettle and bring to a boil. Reduce the heat to a gentle simmer and cook for 15–20 minutes, or until the apples are tender but not falling apart.
5. Remove the crab apples from the hot syrup and put aside. Repeat with the remaining half of the crab apples.
6. When all the crab apples have been cooked, remove the kettle from the heat and return the first batch to the hot syrup.
7. Allow the apples to cool in the syrup.
8. Drain the crab apples, discard the spices, return the syrup to the pan, and bring to the boil.
9. Pack the crab apples into pint or quart jars, cover with the boiling syrup to within ¼ inch of the tops, and screw on the lids.
10. Process for 20 minutes in a boiling water bath.

APPLE MARMALADE

PREPARATION TIME: 60 MINUTES   COOKING TIME: APPROXIMATELY 2 HOURS
YIELD: APPROXIMATELY 8 PINTS

2 medium-size oranges (1 pound)
2 medium-size lemons (½ pound)
1 grapefruit (½ pound)
6 medium-size tart apples (2 pounds) (Twenty Ounce, Rhode Island Greening, Granny Smith)
12 cups water
5 pounds extra fine sugar

1. Scrub the oranges, lemons, and grapefruit. Thinly pare the rinds with a potato peeler or paring knife, making sure to avoid the inner white skin. Remove the white fluffy skin with your fingers and discard.
2. Chop or shred the thin rinds. Place in a large kettle.
3. Squeeze the juice and pips into a bowl. Cut out the inner membranes and chop coarsely. Place in the center of a double piece of cheesecloth along with the pips. Pour the juice into the pan with the shredded rind.
4. Wash, peel, and core the apples. Add the parings to the cheesecloth and tie. Add to the kettle.
5. Chop the apples and add to the kettle with the water.
6. Bring to a boil, reduce the heat, and simmer for about 1½ hours. The peel should be tender and the liquid reduced by approximately half.
7. Lift the cheesecloth bag, squeeze the juice out into the kettle, and discard.
8. Add the sugar and stir until it is completely dissolved.
9. Bring to the boil and continue boiling rapidly until a sugar thermometer registers 220°F. (about 15–20 minutes), or until the marmalade sets when dropped onto a chilled saucer.
10. Skim off the foam and ladle into 8 hot, clean pint-size jars, leaving ½ inch head space. Wipe the rim and cap each one immediately. Process for 10 minutes in a boiling water bath.

APPLE-HERB JELLY

10 medium-size tart apples
5½ cups water
2 cups cider vinegar
7½ cups sugar
6–8 sprigs fresh rosemary,
    tarragon, or lemon thyme or 1
    tablespoon dried herbs

1. Quarter the apples and place in a large kettle with the water and cider vinegar. Simmer for 30 minutes, or until the apples are soft.
2. Pour the fruit and liquid into a sieve or colander lined with 4 layers of cheesecloth or into a dampened jelly bag and strain. Allow to drip for 2–3 hours. For a clear jelly, do not press the fruit.
3. Measure 4 cups of juice into a clean kettle and bring to the boil. Add ¾ cup sugar for each cup of liquid and boil for 10 minutes or until the sugar has dissolved and 220°F. registers on a jelly thermometer. The jelly should set when dropped onto a chilled saucer. During this boiling process, remove the leaves from the stems of the herbs.
4. Remove the jelly from the heat when it jells and skim off the foam. Add a drop of green vegetable coloring, if desired, and the fresh or dried herbs. Stir and pour immediately into 8 hot, sterilized jelly jars, leaving ⅛ inch head room and seal with 2-piece metal canning lids. Or leave ¼ inch head room and cover immediately with a ⅛-inch layer of melted paraffin.
5. Repeat the process until all the liquid has been used.

MINT APPLE JELLY

PREPARATION TIME: 60 MINUTES, PLUS 2–3 HOURS DRIP TIME   YIELD: APPROXIMATELY 4 HALF-PINTS

10 medium-size tart apples
3 cups water
2 cups fresh mint leaves
3 tablespoons lemon juice
3 cups sugar

For plain apple jelly, omit the mint leaves and add two sticks of cinnamon.

1. Quarter the apples and place in a large kettle with the water and mint. Simmer for 30 minutes or until the apples are soft.
2. Pour the fruit and liquid into a sieve or colander lined with 4 layers of cheesecloth or into a dampened jelly bag and strain. Allow to drip for 2–3 hours. For a clear jelly, do not press the fruit.
3. Measure the juice into a clean kettle (there should be about 4 cups) and bring to a boil. Add the lemon juice and 3 cups of sugar (¾ cup sugar per cup of juice). Boil for 10 minutes or until the sugar has dissolved and 220°F. registers on a jelly thermometer. The jelly should set when dropped onto a chilled saucer.
4. When the jell stage has been reached, skim off the foam. Add a drop of green vegetable coloring, if desired. Pour immediately into 4 hot, sterilized jelly jars, leaving ⅛ inch head space and seal with a 2-piece metal cap. Or leave ¼ inch head space and seal immediately with a ⅛ inch layer of melted paraffin.

DRYING APPLES

Sun-drying, an extremely popular method of food preservation in colonial times, has been a mode of food preservation since the Stone Age. The easiest way to dry apples, however, is to use a food dehydrator or a regular oven.

Apple Slices

1. Choose firm, not-so-juicy, bruise-free apples. Wash the apples if you want the skin left on; otherwise, peel, core, and slice into ¼-inch pieces.
2. Arrange in layers (no more than ½ inch deep) on drying trays. In a dehydrator or a regular oven, dry at temperatures between 120°F. and 140°F. At 140°F. (higher temperatures bake the slices) it will take approximately 6 hours for the slices to dry thoroughly. If you want to do it overnight, set the temperature at 120°F.
3. For evenly dried slices, turn them occasionally on the trays.

Leather Roll-ups

In colonial days, leathers were made by cooking fruits and sugar into a thick sauce and then spreading the mixture thinly over plates. These were then placed in the sun for several hours and finished off in a cooling oven after the baking had been done. Today, leathers are made with cooked or pureed raw fruit, and dried in a dehydrator or regular oven.

APPLE LEATHER

PREPARATION TIME: 15 MINUTES   DRYING TIME IN GAS OVEN: APPROXIMATELY 4 HOURS   YIELD: 2 LARGE ROLLS

4 medium-size apples (Jonathan, Northern Spy, Stayman, Winesap)
1 tablespoon lemon juice
2 tablespoons honey (or to taste)
½ teaspoon ground cinnamon

1. Peel, core, and slice the apples. Place in a food processor or blender.
2. Add the rest of the ingredients and process to a puree. There will be approximately 3 cups of puree.
3. Line 2 jelly roll pans with waxed paper and spread with the apple puree so that it is about ¼ inch thick and comes to within ½ inch of the edges.
4. Place in a 140°F. oven and test after 3 hours. The leather should be slightly sticky and pull away from the waxed paper. Lift up about 1 inch and start rolling it over. Leave whole, or cut into 2 pieces.
5. Store at room temperature for up to 1 month or in the refrigerator or freezer for longer periods.

APPENDIXES

Many a time, the urge to throw a party has been squashed because of all the preparation involved. One of the easiest ways around this is to choose an apple, cheese, and wine theme. Accompany the apples, cheeses, and wines with an assortment of crusty breads, water biscuits, and crackers.

A visit to the local orchards to procure a selection of fresh autumn apples is the first step. Next, choose the cheeses and wines. Identify each apple variety and stack them in baskets next to those cheeses and wines that are considered complementary.

Here's a list of apples and the cheese and wines that have an affinity for each other.

Cortland. Serve with Chèvres (goat cheese), Cheshire, Wensleydale, and Cantal cheeses. Accompany by Codorniu brut (Spanish sparkling), Chablis, Saint Veran, Saint Romaine white wines.

Golden Delicious. Serve with Edam, mild Cheddar, Camembert, and Brie cheeses. Accompany by Medoc and Beaujolais red wines.

Red Delicious; Ida Red. Serve with Roquefort and Saga blue cheeses. Accompany by Chianti or Beaujolais Villages red wines.

Empire. Serve with Muenster, Fontina, Bel Paese cheeses. Accompany by Soave white and rose wines.

Jonagold. Serve with Romano and Gorgonzola cheeses. Accompany by Chianti Borolo, Barbera, Barberesco, and Spanna red wines.

Jonathan. Serve with Scottish Dunlop (Cheddar) Gruyère, and Provolone cheeses. Accompany by Bardolino and Valpolicella red wines, and Orvieto and Vouvray white wines.

Jonamac; McIntosh. Serve with sharp Cheddar and blue Stilton cheeses. Accompany by Spanish Rioja red and port wines.

Macoun. Serve with Caprice des Dieux, Excelsior, Boursault cheeses. Accompany by Moselle, Graves, Pouilly white wines, and red Côte de Beaune.

Northern Spy. Serve with Italian Parmesan, Roquefort, Pont l'Eveque, other blue cheeses. Accompany by St. Emilion, Côtes de Rhone, Fleurie, and Brouilly red wines.

When selecting your apples, be prepared to experiment when a recommended variety is not available or is not in peak condition. Any of the good eaters will taste delicious with cheese, and you may have your own ideas on suitable combinations. Also, don't feel obliged to serve only wine. Try a sampling of fruity and light beers, cider, or Calvados (which is a little smoother than applejack).

Thousands of apple varieties evolved in the United States during the 17th, 18th, and 19th centuries when colonial farmers decided to plant apple seeds instead of young apple tree shoots, or scions, which would arrive from England and Europe. It was thus they

found that the seed of an apple did not produce a tree of the same original variety. It was also during the 18th and 19th centuries that apple seeds were spread from coast to coast by the legendary Johnny Appleseed. Born John Chapman in 1774, in Massachusetts, he traveled the new territories for forty-odd years selling seeds and plants.

The demise of certain apple strains was inevitable. With thousands of varieties to be eaten and sold, those that spoiled quickly were considered a bad risk. By the turn of the 20th century, when transportation became more reliable and all manner of food was available from different areas of the country and various parts of the globe, the heavy reliance on homegrown and local food was drastically diminished. No longer was the home orchard the main source of fruit. Consequently, it was no longer practical to grow such a wide variety of apple trees that had to be pruned, fertilized, and protected from birds and insects. Only those that produced apples judged to be good keepers, the best for making pies, sauce, and cider, were cultivated. Apples that could not stand up to shipping and long storage were discontinued, as were trees that did not bear their first crop for ten years and then only every other year thereafter. Also neglected were those apples with rough, brownish, or mottled skins, deemed to be aesthetically unacceptable to the American public.

Another important element contributed to the elimination of some apple varieties. In 1918, the ravages of a severe winter took its toll on thousands of apple trees in the East. In starting over, commercial orchard growers followed the recommendations of pomologists and planted an abundance of McIntosh, Red Delicious, Golden Delicious, and Rome Beauties.

However, such old-time favorites as Wealthy, Tolman Sweet, Pound Sweet, Rhode Island Greening, and Baldwin can still be found in some of the smaller commercial orchards whose demand is local rather than nationwide.

Indeed, I consider it a lucky day when I stumble upon an old-fashioned orchard, where the gardener prefers flavor to abundance. Such varieties can be a revelation—not only in taste, but also in name and appearance.

Sops of Wine. With white, red-flecked flesh that resembles bread dipped in wine, this apple has a pedigree that goes all the way back to medieval England.

Chenango Strawberry. This originated in New York in the mid-1800s, and is a pale yellow apple with pink stripes. The soft flesh has a distinct strawberry fragrance.

Baldwin. This apple originated in Wilmington, Massachusetts, around 1740. Grown mostly in New York state and New England, it is no longer popular with commercial growers because it takes about 10 years to bear fruit, and then does so only biannually. It is a large red apple, streaked with yellow. The flesh is firm, crisp, juicy, moderately tart, and aromatic. This is a good all-purpose apple.

Black Gilliflower or Sheepnose. This apple, discovered in Connecticut in the late 1700s, has the shape of a sheep's nose and deep, purple red skin. The flesh is firm, sweet, and fragrant. It is delicious for eating out of hand and can also be used for baking.

Cox Orange Pippin. "Pipin" was a common term for a small apple when this one originated in England, around 1830. It is wonderfully aromatic with a rather rough, deep yellow skin that is splashed with orange and red. The flesh is crisp, tender, and fragrantly juicy, making it one of the best dessert apples. It also makes choice cider.

Duchess of Oldenburg. First imported to England in 1815 from Russia, this apple was brought to the United States in 1835. Its tender, red-striped skin encases yellow-tinged flesh. Crisp, firm, and juicy, it is highly rated for pies and sauces, but considered too tart for eating out of hand.

Fameuse or Snow. Originating in France, this has been grown in New York and Vermont since around 1700. It is small and firm with bright red, sometimes purple, skin. Its snow-white, crisp flesh may be striped with red. Excellent for eating raw in desserts and salads, it does not hold its shape during cooking.

Lady. This small apple originated in France during medieval times. With its red and green skin and firm, crisp, white flesh, it is very much in demand around the Christmas season for table decorations. It is delicious to eat fresh and makes good cider.

Porter. A large yellow apple splashed with red, it originated in Massachusetts, around 1800. Its firm, white flesh is crisp, tender, and flavorful. It is ideal for canning, cooking, and eating raw.

Pound Sweet or Pumpkin Sweet. This apple originated in Connecticut, around 1850. It is very large with green-on-yellow striped skin. The flesh is yellow and juicy with an unusual and rather sweet flavor. It is good for baking.

Red Astrachan. This apple reached the United States from Russia around 1835. Its pale yellow skin is splashed with bluish-red stripes and the juicy, white flesh is often tinged with red. An early summer apple that ripens unevenly and does not keep well, it is used for cooking before it is fully mature. However, when ripe, it is excellent for eating fresh in desserts and salads.

Rhode Island Greening. This variety originated around 1700 from a chance seed found growing outside a Rhode Island tavern owned by a Mr. Green of Green's End, Newport. The bright green skin surrounds flesh that is crisp, juicy, and tart. If allowed to ripen, they became mellow enough to be eaten out of hand. However, most orchardists pick them "green," which makes them a perfect pie apple.

Roxbury Russet. A real American oldie that originated in Roxbury, Massachusetts, around 1635. Its gold skin is mottled with flecks of brown and red; the crisp yellow flesh is deliciously sweet. Excellent for eating fresh and making into cider, it also has a long storage life.

Smokehouse. William Gibbons grew this apple near his smokehouse during the early 19th century, in Lancaster County, Pennsylvania. Its yellowish-green skin is mottled with red and the creamy flesh is firm and juicy, making it a good candidate for fresh desserts and the salad bowl. It is not recommended for cooking.

Summer Rambo. One of the older varieties, it originated in France, where it was called the Rambour France, and was introduced into the United States in 1817. This large apple is greenish-yellow with red stripes. The tender, juicy flesh makes it ideal for eating fresh and making into sauce.

Tolman Sweet. The origin of this apple is said to be Dorchester, Massachusetts, around 1822. Its greenish-yellow skin is sometimes blushed with light pink. The white flesh is exceptionally sweet and it is considered the best for making naturally sweet apple sauce. It is also good for baking and eating fresh.

Tompkins King. Discovered in New Jersey around 1800, it is a large, yellow apple splashed with broad, red stripes. The skin is tender and the creamy flesh crisp, juicy, and moderately tart. Not a favorite for eating fresh, it is best used for cooking.

Twenty Ounce. Thought to have originated in Connecticut, it was first exhibited in Massachusetts around 1845. A large, green apple which is splashed with red stripes when ripe, its firm, tart flesh is encased in tough skin. This combination makes it superb for cooking.

Wealthy. This thin-skinned, pale yellow apple, heavily shaded with red, was discovered in Minnesota, around 1860. Its crisp, juicy white flesh is often streaked with red. An excellent apple for eating fresh, for cooking, and for making cider.

Westfield Seek-No-Further. At one time considered the finest of dessert apples, this one originated in Westfield, Massachusetts, around 1796. The skin of this yellowish-green apple is splashed with red, and the pale yellow flesh is crisp, juicy, and flavorful.

Winter Banana. Another 100-year-old variety, this orginated in Indiana, has pink-on-yellow cheeks, and, not surprisingly, a flavor reminiscent of bananas.

Wolf River. Named after Wolf River in Wisconsin, where it was found, the date of origin is placed around 1880. It is an oversized apple and stories abound in which only one was necessary for a pie. Its skin is pale yellow, heavily streaked with red, and the light yellow flesh is firm, tender, and juicy. Excellent for eating fresh and cooking.

INDEX